ESCAPE TO FREEDOM

VAH BENJAMIN KELLY

Thank for reading
—Uncle Nat—

8-13-2023

Published by

www.improved2life.com

Author's Contact

Email: vah_kelly@yahoo.com

Facebook: Vah Kelly

My wife, Dorothy you are priceless and highly chosen

To my four children, Benjamin, Zonetta, Tarena, and Natalie.

To my parents, Joe & Etta,

thanks for the prayer and support.

My in-laws, especially Mama Zondell,

together with Harriet, Malcolm, and the family, including my

beloved nephew Shawn. May the blessings

of our ancester Abraham be yours.

Watchien and Rufus my support arms thanks for being there.

For the unknown kids who were lost due to the

plight of the Liberian civil conflict, may your souls rest in peace.

You are amazing in the Lord!

My prayer buddies, Charles and Kamara, thanks for being

there when I needed you most!

Keep the faith to continue trusting and believing

in God, and don't you dare give up on

God, for He has not given up on you.

*When we put our trust in a place where trust cannot
find itself, then we must lean and depend on
a higher power to lead us through.....Vah*

*For the Lord has chosen Jacob to be his own,
Israel to be his treasured possession.*
Psalm 135:4

CONTENTS

PREFACE

This book was written to highlight the message of hope, faith, and trust in God as the ultimate source of inspiration. It also gives light to the destiny of a believer. When all other grounds around us become unstable, there is hope in Jesus Christ. It is a true story based on the demonstration of God's love and protection of a stubborn believer's life as he goes through the terrible struggle of survival while trying to avoid the calling on his life as a disciple of Christ. Life is an art: some would say that we must envisage and decide on the pattern and shape to bring out the brighter side of every crafted piece as humans. We planned and made promises because of ignorance, unaware of what the next second or minute even holds. Such is life as we learn and live to honor this world where travel never ceases. We take on an endless journey to find happiness and prosperity while avoiding what should be important in our lifetime duty: commitment towards the calling of God. You were chosen since the day of birth as stated in the book of the prophet Jeremiah 1:5, which reads: "Before I form thee in the belly, I have known thee; and before thou comest forth from the womb I have sanctified thee, a prophet to nations."

Instead of serving and becoming obedient to God's will, we embark on the journey of a lifetime performing duties outside of our calling. In return, life takes us into unknown places depending on the situation, including trials, circumstances, and tribulations. As the Moses said, we spend our lives like a tale that is told. *"For all our days are passed away in thy wrath: we spend our years as a tale that is told" (Psalm 90:9).*

INTRODUCTION

Our lives are filled with the mysteries of this world. At some point, we have all experienced events that cannot be explained or understood. Some of these occurrences tend to question the border of our minds and the future implications. We tend to ask about the reason for our birth and the family from whom we were brought forth. The tragedies we have gone through and the outcome make us wonder why such tragedies should occur. Should bad things happen to good people? There remain unanswered questions that we might never know and find very difficult to comprehend. They may be physical or spiritual, but as we draw nearer to God, He begins to reveal His purpose for us to understand why He created us.

We may not understand how God works at times, but it is true that He does work and will meet us when we need Him most. There is never a useless prayer, and we should not be discouraged when things do not go according to our plans. God is a rewarder of those who diligently seek His face, and He will supply every need of ours according to His riches in glory.

Prayer can be compared to going on an assigned job and performing tasks designated to you daily. You sign in and begin work with the assurance that you will get paid at the end of the pay period. When we pray and seek the face of God, making requests, we know that our prayers will be answered only if we can wait on God's time. As believers, praying should become a habit, not occasional or performed only when we need God. We should seek His face daily by asking for His direction, and through faith, He will supply all our needs.

Clarence says he has been through a lot and wondered at times if there was a God at all. "If God is the creator of heaven and earth, why do bad things happen to good people? How did He allow us to get this far in destroying ourselves and behaving as monsters by killing people?" He wondered. The world has changed, and he wondered if things would ever be the same as they were. Friends have turned into foes while boys and girls were turned into fighting people at war, going forward without guidance. He screamed that our nation was in trouble and prayed that God would intervene and save the state. But his prayers were never answered as expected. He got angry and began to regret why he went to church and worship on Sundays. Where was the God of Abraham, Isaac, and Jacob when he needed Him most? Our God is awesome and a pleasant help in times of trouble.

Chapter 1
THE BEGINNING

Clarence Franklin is his name, and he was born into a beautiful middle-class family in Liberia and lived with his siblings under one roof. His parents desired to give him the best in education though they had no college degree; they wanted the best for their children. His folks were born in the countryside, with both of his parents having little formal education, but they became educated later in life and taught him the importance of family. He remembered growing up and attending elementary and senior high schools in the city of Monrovia though living in the suburbs. His parents wanted the best quality education, which came at a price. The wages earned were minimum, but they had a roof over their heads and a place to call home. Clarence's father had a car that transported them to school daily, and all they had to do was to study and make the pass in every class.

Things were fine as kids. All they needed was to attend class, and after school and during the weekend or school break, they could play with their friends. Of course, they were required to attend church service every Sunday at an Anglican church because the priest knew their parents and would surely ask why they did not attend church service. He would notice their absence during the blessings of the kids. This was a community church, the priest knew everyone attending the church. Later in his childhood, Clarence explained about an attack from people using witchcraft activities and appearing in his dreams. He experienced difficulties sleeping alone with the lights turned off and had to be watched daily by an adult. He would go to bed and see snakes all over his bed when the lights were off while sleeping alone. This was terrifying for a child and made him cry at night for help. He remembered at times that his mother would jump out of bed and run to his room to inquire about what was happening. But it was spiritual; she did not have such eyes to see the horror taking place behind the scenes. The enemies wanted Clarence dead before he could even grow up. They might have known something that he was never aware of and were determined to get what they wanted. He struggled psychologically as a child then, when no one could see what he saw, and at times his father would think that he was faking things for attention. But his mother knew what was happening and tried to find a solution. He could recall that before the rededication of his mother to Christianity, he was taken to a fetish priest to inquire what was going on. Clarence recalls telling his mother that it was a dragon (a form of African witchcraft appearing as a snake) that was behind his attack and

4

wanted him dead to hurt his mother. Why was that important? He had no clue. It was prefer for the witches to answer.

Growing up in the township of Samukai was all that he knew, and he had everything a child would need to be happy. He attended a well-disciplined boarding institution in the early '80s, made friends, and learned the way of life from others. It was his first encounter outside of their family home after attending elementary school in the city. He was growing up fast, and his parents, particularly his dad, wanted him to be strong and learn the reality of life that other boys went through.

While in boarding school, the desire to become an Anglican priest was strong. Later Clarence got baptized and confirmed by an archbishop at the time. But soon, he began falling into disciplinary problems, fighting, and sometimes not following instructions. Of course, there were disciplinary actions meant to keep him grounded. The year went by quickly, and most of his peer group left the institution because of hardship, but he decided to remain with the older boys and ended the academic year successfully. The following year, he returned to the city and enrolled at another school, where he finished high school and graduated. The early '80s were good years, and life was fun and filled with excitement with a prosperous future ahead. Clarence and his friends hung out around the township and neighborhood for hours while awaiting the beginning of another academic season to join either college or university.

In a township like theirs, everybody knew one another, and they were considered children of the community. Discipline was high, and their parents' friends could serve as their father or mother to correct their actions if caught misbehaving in public. Clarence grew up as a devoted Christian and attended church service almost seven days a week, with his mother being a member of the Pentecostal Church. He also attended monthly fast, including weekly Bible studies, and sang in the choir. He and his siblings were taught to trust and believe in God for their needs, and they took time to clean the church for Sunday's service, amongst other things. All the excitement changed on December 24, 1989, with the firing of the first gun of a group of rebels and mercenaries that would change his life forever. Rebels launched an attack against the government through a border town in the north of the country. He was in the city of Monrovia on an early morning when he saw thousands of displaced people walking from one place to another, seeking refuge. It was funny at first, and stories were told about how abusive government soldiers were and that the rebels had magical powers. They knew nothing about the war other than what was seen on the television of war heroes and combat movies made by Hollywood. But the country was gradually crawling into another thing, leading them into a decade of one of Africa's brutal civil conflicts claiming over 150,000 lives.

The invaders had one demand in mind: the immediate resignation of the country's president, and the country would return to civilians. It was the first in Liberia's history, and imagine he was just out of high school, inexperienced to what was unveiled before his eyes. The president had loyal and strong forces but decided to host a series of negotiation meetings with the rebels in joint consolidation with regional bodies to reach an agreement. After negotiations failed, the rebels began an assault on the capital city, Monrovia, and it was brutal. Both day and night were dreadful, with unlawful arrests and executions by government forces in the capital city and environs. Rebel and government forces were committing atrocities outside the capital city as well as executing humans by the thousands. Clarence lived in the suburbs outside Monrovia and saw an increase in security checkpoints and unnecessary arrests, including the detention of peaceful civilians.

His expectations after high school graduation were the dream of joining a university and becoming what you wanted as a professional; to start life, look for a job, and begin a family. The situation was confusing, and he thought it would end in a matter of days as there were other uprisings before, like the 1979 and 1980 coup, which brought the Tolbert regime to an end and ushered in a military government to power. There was another attempted invasion to unseat the same government. It was a familiar scene at first when it came to news of armed men shooting, but this one was different. Never had he seen thousands of citizens fleeing and seeking refuge within the country's border.

Clarence visited a friend, Patrick, along Gardnerville Road and had to walk a long way because of the shortage of transportation. After a lengthy conversation with his friend, he bid him farewell and walked away. Later, during the week, he learned that while his friend was returning home, he had a slight misunderstanding with a government army officer and got shot in the leg multiple times. Praise be given to God that he survived and is a man of God today, sharing the truth about his faith in God. The grace of God will always protect you once you have faith and trust in Him as it is written:

"God is our refuge and strength,
a very present help in trouble"
(Psalm 46:1)

As we often go through circumstances, we might not be able to see the manifestation of God calling upon our lives. But not every trial or temptation that we experience appears to destroy us; it is something that we should be aware of. Some circumstances are meant to remold us and refine our existence by renewing our faith in God.

Clarence gathered the courage to remain calm despite those happenings and went through the moment in fear. Later, what would occur would send a chill through him and set a memory that would unlikely go away. While in the township, they had fun and laughter amidst life's uncertainties. A civil war was gradually taking place, and the country was slipping into anarchy. They took the opportunity to have fun when the authorities ran for shelter under the pretense of going for a vacation or peace talks taking family members secretly along. Deception was the order of the day in Monrovia among the authorities, who were aware of the strength of the rebel's forces but kept quiet because of fear of reprisal from within. What's worst was that house helps and maidservants, among others, were left unaware as their masters fled with their immediate family members leaving them to keep watch over properties and personal belongings.

He felt that those left behind to take care of properties should have been told something in advance to keep them safe. For these reasons, innocent lives were lost because of the campaign launched by the rebels and government forces executing civilians because of false allegations against those poor souls betrayed by their masters. Is it true that the sins of the fathers follow the children? One may wonder. Servants were made to account for the deeds of their masters that they were unaware of while the masters escaped into neighboring countries for safety. The need for God as our pleasant help in times of trouble and uncertainty can never be underemphasized. The war was brutal, with thousands already killed and more executed because of tribal affiliation and decades of silly tribal conflict left unresolved. It is dangerous, especially when a nation keeps ignoring certain minorities by failing to adequately address sensitive issues, and things are secretly swept under the carpet instead of bringing it to an end with all parties concerned. Failure to give attention and bring an amicable ending to a situation will breathe disunity and uncertainties among the party's concerns. The future generation is left with the task of solving what their ancestors did not solve, creating disunity among the community and breaking interfamily ties.

The battle for control of the capital of Monrovia continued, and many other youths got confused as they had never traveled out of the country since birth and were also afraid to follow the crowd seeking refuge. Clarence noticed his folks were not making a move. Though afraid, he trusted that God would deliver them from every circumstance. The situation was deteriorating at night, with government forces randomly firing, trying to create awareness of their presence in the area. Clarence's cousin Toliver resided at another relative's house who had secretly fled the country. He was an official of the government assigned to the security area. He left Toliver to watch over his family property. It was on a fatal evening in July 1990 when Clarence went over, and they decided to have a few drinks and cook a meal while at home. Gladly, the bodyguard Sgt. Sabastine Weah was around and told them that everything was okay, and his boss had asked him to do a periodic check on the property. But he wanted more than just to have fun in the house and requested them to invite some female friends and go to a bar for the evening. What could they say? He was in charge and had the cash, being a senior member of the military.

Clarence decided to spend the night. The gathering was quick, and connections were made with the females to take a ride with them to a drinking spot for a few drinks. The decision to go out was a terrible mistake, and we did not see it coming. Sgt. Weah, as he was called, told the driver Manjo, another agent of the Joint Security Force, to drive them to the spot for a night of excitement. There was a railroad track on the other side of the main motorway. The sergeant instructed the driver to take the back road instead of the main road. Clarence can still recall where the incident took place, and it was barely ten minutes after they drove from the house. All that he heard was "HALT!" shouted a soldier of the government forces. It was too late to stop. Before Manjo could apply the brake, a soldier had opened fire on a government vehicle using a government-issued machine gun. The sergeant decided to get down and identify himself during the firing. But the soldier, being afraid, decided to continue firing inside the vehicle, and the sergeant's head was riddled with bullets killing him instantly. Clarence sat by him and leaned forward, crying his heart out together with the girls who were in the car, afraid of being hit with a bullet. Suddenly, he felt something like lukewarm water running down his neck. The sergeant had been killed, and parts of his brain were all over his hair, even stuck on his shirt. Clarence told his cousin, Toliver, "This is a moment for survival." He sensed that they could all be executed once the government forces realized that a soldier had killed a ranking officer.

The site where the incident took place was near a community high school. A cassava patch was nearby, and they decided to run into it for refuge. They could still hear behind them the conversation between government soldiers and the driver Manjo after the firing had ceased. They were asking the driver for his identity. After identifying who he was, the driver was instructed to turn the car around and return home. We were frightened and ran home; we even had to jump the fence to get into the house though we had the keys to the gate. We could barely sleep when the driver returned to the compound, and we saw that the car windows had been shattered because of bullets. But what's worse was the brain of Sgt. Sabastine Weah stuck to the ceiling and seats of the car, making this night unbearable. The scent was awful, and we had to clean up the vehicle that night; the blood and brains! Only God knows. Clarence was seated next to the guy who got killed, and not a single bullet hit him. What was going on? *We could have been killed, and nobody would know what had taken place. There must be a God somewhere out there and a reason for protecting me.* What was His reason for protecting me? he thought, unable to comprehend, still confused. Then he knew that the hands of God were upon him.

Early the next morning, with his shirt filled with blood because of the previous night, he decided to walk the same route, as it was a Sunday morning, and see what the scene was like in the daylight. He did not get far enough as the soldier had realized by then that a ranking officer had been killed the previous night and was in the process of removing the body. They prevented folks from using the route that morning until they cleared the human remains. He quickly ran home and told his folks what had occurred the previous night. His parents were mad at him and asked why he had to leave the house, warning him of the further danger with the presence of soldiers in the area. After a while, his dad said it was dangerous for him to be at home and wanted the rest of the family to be protected from reprisal should they decide to carry out an investigation and need state witnesses. He had to leave for another relative's place, his mother's younger sister's residence. Again, after explaining what had previously occurred, he was asked to leave because her husband was another security personnel with the police unit.

It seemed like he was running from one place to another in search of shelter and safety, but he knew that God had a plan for him somewhere, so the journey continued to another relative's place. There, he finally found rest with his cousin and shared a room with him. For days, people were moving from one place to another with unpleasant looks on their faces, sharing stories of distress. During the day, he would walk miles into the bushes, seeking food to eat. "We fed on wild yam and palm cabbage," said Clarence. He wondered where they were heading as restless days and nights passed with the shelling of mortar guns by both the government troop and rebel forces trying to take over the 72nd military barracks.

His thoughts were on his folks back at home as he tried many times to go through the swamp but was prevented by government soldiers at checkpoints. The road back to his home in Coffee Farm seemed to be closed because of the rebel presence, and he was so afraid of being caught by the rebels after hearing terrifying stories of torture and unwanted executions from rebel-controlled areas.

After weeks of uncertainties, there was a breakthrough with news that the rebel forces had left because of rumors that another fearful group of rebels was advancing but not alone; they took hostages as a human shield. "The leader of the incoming rebels, Prince Johnson, will execute you guys if you decide to remain here," said Charles Taylor's fleeing rebels to civilians. Later, they found out it was all a lie, as folks became aware that the fighting men were afraid of encountering Johnson's fierce men in battle because of his success in rebel warfare. Clarence decided to be brave and take the road through the swamp with the thought of either running into government forces or the rebel group. Living in fear without seeing his family was no longer an option. He needed to see his child and his mother, were also captured under the rebel stronghold but had been released. Coming through the swamp, he encountered no one until he reached the end of the path and heard voices of folks trying to recover after rebels held ordeals. There were stories of rape, torture, and daily execution of former government officials, including security personnel, on the hostage site.

14

Children were abducted from their parents to be used as child soldiers by rebel fleeing forces, contributing to the men's power of the rebels. But the end was yet to come as he met his young son and his mother, looking dehydrated and tired. She narrated the ordeal in a rebel-held area, and one could see the trauma on her face. They decided to move back to the family house and leave the vicinity before the rebels returned that day, but they did not. The following morning, Clarence and a neighbor decided to walk along with the other displaced and returning residents over two miles to the market center of the island to purchase necessities, including food for the house. They began to talk about their ordeal and share lessons learned from past activities when, suddenly, a soldier of the government forces asked them to come over for questioning. They walked over, and he said that they should sit on the ground and asked them for their identity cards. Victor presented his university student ID card, while Clarence presented an ordinary passport.

Victor was wrongly accused of being a supporter of the rebels, being a student at the University of Liberia, known in the past to stage riots in response to government injustices, among other things. Likewise, Clarence was given the charge of not being patriotic enough and wanting to flee the country after not signing up to fight in a time of danger. There would be no escape, and they wondered what the next action of the soldier would be. Suddenly, there was gunfire coming from the other side, and he quickly gave back their documents and asked them to leave at once.

"For in the time of trouble he shall hide me in his pavilion: in the secret of his tabernacle shall he hide me; he shall set me up upon a rock"
(Psalm 27:5 NIV)

God had indeed given them shelter under His wings, and they were not harmed.

They walked and got in line with the others who were walking towards the city center, seeing mutilated human remains along the road and dogs eating the flesh of their former masters (humans) for food. There were other soldiers along the route who did not bother stopping them as they went along their way. Finally, they were able to reach their destination and got the necessities while thinking about which road to take going back home. The fear of meeting with those soldiers and falling into another nightmare was the highlight of their thoughts. They met other people with similar fear, who explained how they avoided the soldiers by taking another bypass route over the river using a canoe ride for a little charge. Clarence was afraid of the river as he had never rode a canoe. However, the courage to reunite with his family was a priority and a risk worth taking.

He prayed and asked the Lord God to take charge as they entered the canoe, agreeing to the term of the operator. While the canoe navigated across the river, fear was in him as the water began to enter the canoe, and they were told to help in getting it out. Panic hit him in the middle of the river when the canoe began to rock, and it seemed at first that all hope was lost. But he guessed that it was the current of the river. They finally hit the shore, thanks to God. They compensated the operator and headed back through the back route to their homes. Clarence knew the route that they took, but not the river part, as a distant relative of his mother lived there, and his grandmother usually visited them for family moments. Of course, the road leading there involved passing through a forest, and folks had a saying that there was an older man who once lived there who turned into a dwarf at nights and would whip the living hell out of passersby.

He was caught, by the authorities accused of practicing withcraft.The place became abandoned after that but had fruits like mango trees and oranges planted on the property. They walked through the bushes and finally came to the house, where they decided to leave the area because of the fear of the government soldiers and what they had experienced. The night passed, and there were sounds of guns firing from a distance throughout the night. He could not wait till dawn and barely slept, thinking of what he had been through and was so afraid of what might occur should the rebels and the government clash again. The next morning, Lorenzo and Clarence decided to leave the area, but his neighbor made up his mind to remain and watch over his family property, being the older child. They parted and headed toward the city center again for safety because of fear of an attack. Where should they go? There was another neighbor who had gotten married and moved out of the area not too far from the power plant on Bushrod Island. The amazing thing was that grace was upon them while they traveled, as those soldiers along the road did not ask any questions.

It reminded Clarence of the Bible and the story of Daniel and how the lions' mouths were shut when he placed them into the lions' den. This must be an amazing grace, and God was carrying them through the line of blood-thirsty soldiers armed to their teeth, willing to kill at any time. Upon reaching their temporary destination, their hosts gave them a room and told them to rest. There, they spent the night and decided to seek shelter in a displaced camp, afraid of an attack by the rebels seeking control of the only existing power plant in the country. Again, the government forces were all over the place in numbers, but there were also civilians traveling with children and personal belongings along the way. At night, there was a curfew, and people were told to be off the street due to security concerns.

Lorenzo, Clarence's cousin, worked with the Joint Security Forces of the government and had his ID card hidden with him. The war had begun, and nobody knew whom to trust anymore, so he hid his identity card. Early the next morning, he said to Clarence, "Let us find another shelter, probably a displaced camp." They had only heard the name but had never been there. As they set off that morning, Lorenzo said goodbye to the family and promised to return upon finding a place safe for them. They walked for hours, hungry with neither food to eat nor water to drink. The only source of food was sugar-cane, which they brought along the way. The sight of malnourished children carried on the backs of their mothers was the order of the day. There were also disabled folks carried in wheelbarrows and, at times, died en route, unable to make the journey.

The sight of children feeding on the breast of malnourished mothers was painful, but what could be done as the battle waged on for control of the city? After walking for hours, they were finally at a site considered the Voice of America abandoned compound in Virginia, Liberia. The crowd that had gathered was huge, and more were coming, trying to find a place of refuge. They needed a spot to erect their shelter to sleep, but could it be erected without any building material or equipment? Walking through, they had to ask for vacant space to erect their structures and were given one by those who were there earlier. They had to take turns using other peoples' tools like a machetes, shovels, diggers, and the like. They needed palm branches, sticks, nails, or rope to erect the structure that day.

They only had a day to work because they carried no food or clothes to change into the next day. Secondly, they had to go into the bushes to find materials to construct their structures. Finding it impossible to complete that day, they decided to mark out the given spot, head back to town, get their necessary supplies, and return with their families for the last time. Later that evening, they decided to take a bath and were directed to a place called Adam and Eve Creek, a fictitious name given because of the public display of naked folks where people bathed openly, both male and female. The sight was unbelievable, as both naked men and women bathed in the open area. Clarence was shocked and said to his cousin, "What is this?" But the folks did not mind at all; they had been accustomed to the place. "What was there to be ashamed of anyway?" his cousin asked. Some people had lost everything because of the civil conflict and barely held onto life.

Others had lost family members and property, and the feeling of some dignity had even gone away from them, unsure whether they would see another dawn. The things of this world are temporary, and we should not put our hearts into them. Life should be taken a day at a time, for the future is promised to no one. Here were highly respected folks within the community sleeping on the ground in the open. No amount of money could replace what they were about to experience. Clarence and his cousin put on their brave faces and jumped in the water, taking baths as the night was suddenly fell. They had to sleep because of the curfew and the news of gun exchanges from afar.

Chapter 2
NOWHERE TO HIDE

Clarence and Lorenzo slept in the open with the others who had just arrived and could hear the exchange of gunfire and rocket launches throughout the night. Thanks to God, it did not rain. The next day they decide to leave VOA and head back to town, afraid of what had occurred to their family while they were away. They walked for hours and saw others returning from town too. Upon reaching the bridge, it was a sight to see as government forces were on their side of the bridge and allowed them to cross. As they got to the other side of the bridge, they saw another group of armed men dressed differently, some in sneakers, boots, and slippers. They raised their hands in total surrender but were quickly told to put their hands down and move on as they were not prisoners of war. The rebel soldiers asked if they saw their comrades on the bridge, and they replied in the affirmative.

As they hurried out of the area, in the distance, sounds of gunfire were heard behind them, but thanks be to God that His grace had carried them through. Amazing grace had been with them throughout these situations, but there remained doubts in Clarence's mind about why he was saved from tragedies. It could not have been his goodness or obedience to the God of his fathers, Abraham, Isaac, and Jacob, because he was engulfed in sins.

They were able to reach the family home, and their family had a long explanation of what had occurred during their absence. The fighting that took place between the government forces keeping guard over the power plant and the rebel forces trying to take control of the plant. It lasted for a couple of hours as the government forces fled the area with few left to keep guard because of fear of the rebels' fighting power, led by General Jonson. Clarence needed more information on the area from the direction where his family property was located and how they could return home, seeing a group of people walking toward a bridge that divided the township of Caldwell from the island. The guards of the rebel forces who had captured the area told residents that the road was not yet open to civilians.

After two days, the rebel forces of Prince Johnson decided to open the road and granted residents the liberty to return home. The rebels verified that the area was safe under their control. He decided to head back home with the rest of the family as the road was clear without harassment and intimidation. The moment they turned to the path leading to their house, they met a commander of the rebel forces trying to find a place for displaced people to reside. Vacant homes were broken into and given to displaced people. Clarence narrated that the commander attempted to break into the family home upon reaching his house, and he shouted, "No!" With a strange look on his face, the soldier turned around and asked, very amazed, "Is this your house?" and he replied in the affirmative. He then threatened to execute him if he was lying but was surprised when he took out the keys from his pocket and opened the door to the house.

The soldiers asked Clarence if he would allow displaced people to reside in their homes, and he gave them his condition for acceptance. He could accept two families and no more because of the expectation of his parents' return. It was peacefully settled, and the soldier left them with the promise to bring back food for them. After a few days of heavy fighting, it was reported that Johnson's forces had captured the shipping port and begun supplying food to displaced civilians from the port. They were given two bags of rice, a box of canned chicken, and five gallons of vegetable oil for the house by soldiers distributing food to civilians. What to expect next was unknown. They spent the night in horror as the government launched a series of rockets, and the sounds were so loud.

How could he sleep amid uncertainties? Clarence wondered and was afraid that government soldiers would attack and outrun the forces of the rebels. His thought of being slaughtered like other families in the past grew even more. There was no way out, and he might just get accustomed to being there; after all, it was home. But with these new occupying forces there, nobody knew what to expect.

In the evenings, they were told to gather at a location considered to be their headquarters so that their leader, Johnson, could speak with the civilians. He was a fearful-looking, charismatic leader with an AK 47 rifle lying across his chest and could sing well. He had a guitar in his hand and beautifully sang the song "O How I Love Jesus" and later led us in prayer. Afterward, he gave a daily briefing of his battlefront activities. Then he began to explain the current situation of his forces trying to capture the city. It became a regular evening whenever he returned from the battlefront with his AK-47 rifle and a silver pistol on his side-dress, in a US camouflage uniform. "But what made me afraid," said Clarence, "was the look on his face, unshaved, with white chalk meant as some protective covering, and could not smile at all."

The residents later returned home, and Clarence and his family spent another night in fear, but this night was different from other nights. It was raining, and the sound of rockets being launched by the government forces on the rebel-controlled areas was devastating. It was so loud that the residents had to run outside and lie on the ground, afraid that the rockets would land on their houses.

"This was the funniest sight I had ever seen," Clarence said, beginning to laugh.

"Why are you in the rain?" Clarence asked the head of the family, who was an elderly man. Rockets were fired indiscriminately by government forces toward civilian neighborhood and displaced centers in and around Monrovia.

"Are you not afraid that the rocket would land on the house and kill you?" he openly replied

Clarence said, "Nope."

"You might be brave and not afraid of death," the elderly man replied.

What was there to be afraid of after all that he had been through? He never knew his story, and Clarence was determined not to tell anyone. He only wanted to see his parents and prayed that this whole idea of war would come to an end. Days and weeks passed, and the situation began to settle as it was fully known by now that this could be a long way toward the end. The rebel soldiers became occupational forces in the area, setting up unnecessary checkpoints. They stopped civilians and market people daily, asked questions, and sometimes asked for goods, mainly food items, at their assigned post. People willingly gave in to their requests and felt that they were performing an awesome task by keeping the area safe from Taylor's forces.

As time went by, Clarence received a message from his mother with instructions to get a blanket that was left with a distant relative and send it to her. The road had not been opened yet where she and the rest of the family were, and she needed the blanket. The next morning after taking a shower, he began a journey that should have taken no more than thirty minutes on foot. It was peaceful till he came to another rebel checkpoint and spoke gently with the guys at the location, who asked where he was heading. After a brief conversation, he said, "Thank you, mehn," as commonly said in Liberia, and departed. After retrieving the blanket from his aunt, he was heading back home, passing through the same checkpoint, when he was stopped and asked where the blanket was taken from. Amazed, he replied, "From my aunt," and the commander said that was a lie. He seemed to have been drinking heavily and was unreasonable. Later, the commander instructed him to sit on the ground and threatened him with execution for being a thief and disobedient. He explained that the blanket was taken from his aunt and that he was willing to verify should the commander designate an escort to the home of his aunt, which could be seen from their position. He refused to listen.

"Did you go to school?" he asked.

"Yes," Clarence answered.

"What did you say when you were here earlier?" He then asked

"We spoke, and I was given the green light to move on. I then said, "thank you, mehn' and left. That was it." Clarence said, confused.

"Is 'thank you, mehn' an English word?" He asked.

He was mad and said that Clarence was disobedient to authority. Afraid of being held there till nightfall, he apologized, but the commander would not accept. Then a thought came into Clarence's head that should it get dark, he could be executed, and the family would not know what had occurred. After a few minutes, he told the armed guard left to keep watch over him after his commander, CO Myers, had left that he had a brother who was an officer on the base, in charge of the ammunition building. It was the Holy Spirit directing the thoughts of Clarence at this point because all negotiations had failed. It is written that God is our help in times of trouble. He needed God's intervention and was not giving up on Him for deliverance because He had brought him that far by faith. The armed guard asked, "Are you one of our tribesmen?" Clarence replied, "No, my mother is, but my father is from another tribal group." This was not true at all, but something had to be said in securing a release. The guard said, "Are you sure? Because if you lie, you will be executed." Execution seemed to be the most common word used during the Liberian civil conflict, as all armed men and women took immense pleasure in taking lives away. It became the norm of how human beings have all turned into beasts of the night and need blood as fuel to keep the engine of demonic dominance moving. He had been taught that lying was bad and his parents would punish him for telling lies, but at this point, he needed to tell tales.

Then Clarence remembered that a former neighbor, whom his mother had been nice to his family during good times, had come with the rebel forces. He came and once inquired where the family was, and when he spoke and told him that they had not returned, he told him not to worry but call upon him whenever the need arose.

He told them about him, and you could see the fear on their faces when Clarence told them the story. They spoke in their dialect. He knew right there that his prayer had been answered for God to deliver him out of the hands of wicked and blood thirsty men. The Bible says,

"He shall cover thee with his feathers, and under his wings shalt thou trust: his truth shall be thy shield and buckler"
(Psalm 90:4)

Later, he was escorted to his house by an armed man instructed to shoot him should he attempt to escape. During the walk, the armed man asked again, "Are you sure that Commanding Officer John is your brother?" Clarence said, "yes," and then began to explain his innocence, but the armed man was only taking orders from his boss. Upon reaching the house, he bid Clarence goodbye and thanked him. Still in total shock, he explained the ordeal to his family, and they were terrified.

That week another commander named John, being his alleged brother, drove by to check on him and see if his parents had returned. The story was explained to Commanding Officer John how he was humiliated by the soldier at the checkpoint and accused of being a thief, disrespectful, and threatened with execution. Commander John apologized and said that he might not be able to reach him on time when a situation occurred and offered him a job with the rebels as an unpaid coder. He accepted so that he could defend himself and be recognized as a member of the group. That was important to him, considering what had occurred earlier.

"Are you still involved in the printing work?" He asked.

"Yes," Clarence replied.

"You should be fine then. Let me take you to the headquarters."

Upon mentioning that, his world came crashing down. Afraid, he thought, meeting General Johnson? *What if he executes me?* And thoughts began to fill his head. What better option did he have? Afraid of another rebel coming to the house and attacking his family, he accepted the offer and was taken to the headquarters. Upon arrival at the headquarters, Commander John explained to General Johnson the relationship between them and what he could offer the organization. Instructions were given to prepare military uniforms to be identified as a soldier assigned to the headquarters and begin the preparation of scorpion badges for the rebel forces. The news quickly spread, and the workload was great and began with the general's board of advisers, creating badges for every one of them.

Clarence was placed under the logistics branch as a coding artist assigned to the pool of vehicles. The job description was to design and place a unique numbering system for identifying vehicles under Johnson's areas of control. There were also reports of looting within the city center, with some of his soldiers executed. He witnessed the occasional execution of civilians accused of being from another ethnic group on the deck of a former minister of public works' home, housing the then motor pool. It was getting rampant until the commander of the section reported to General Johnson that it was not in the good image of the organization for a soldier to continue executing people publicly in his assigned area. As time went by, they stopped seeing the execution of civilians in the area. Mornings saw images of dead bodies flooding along the St. Paul river-banks. But that did not stop there, as there was a regular execution spot in the township known for mass execution named "Death Squat Road".

Clarence lived not too far from there, about ten minutes' walk through the bushes. In the evening, they could smell the scent of corpses in the area, which was unbearable. But what could they say, or to whom would they report such environmental and human rights abuses? The area was controlled by Johnson's rebel forces. There was unwanted execution within Johnson's held territory, involving innocent civilians.

Children were turned into soldiers and young men were transformed into fighters and murderers. There was also alcohol and drug abuse while the rebel leader had sex slaves within his compound as well called his wives. It was at this same Death Squat Road that his men executed two well-known US-trained former AFL members, Swen and Karpeh. They were serving as his trainers and were accused of stealing a gallon of vegetable oil. Clarence remembered seeing the lifeless bodies lying in the bushes along the road, with hands tied behind their backs and shot in the head with a single-barrel gun. They would see newly executed bodies every morning or hear gunfire at such locations late in the evenings with execution.

Those grounds hold the voiceless bodies of many who were falsely accused and murdered by angry men of war, at times executed without Johnson's knowledge. The execution ground in the present day, as he learned, was designated as a market ground for the community. Within those surrounding bushes, men and women were shot to death during a senseless civil conflict. Such were the time and conditions then, when men lived in total fear, unaware of what the next moment in life had for them. The soldier who shot and killed the two trainers was considered mentally unfit, yet carried a weapon and could not be persecuted. He was a member of his own ethnic group and had the support of his chief advisers, who sympathized with the soldier's condition. The story behind his madness was that he had shed so much blood earlier during the civil conflict and was partially insane.

There were days when Clarence was threatened by soldiers returning from the frontline who claimed to be commanders to forcibly have their vehicles coded. In times like those, one must be mindful while trusting in a higher power to keep you safe. Living among demons and blood thirsty men who had turned into beasts was frightening. If you were blessed with the gift of seeing the vision, you would see beyond what the ordinary eyes see. They appeared as humans but were demons in desperate need of human blood daily to feed them. Monster of our times, and one must keep high on something to avoid being faint minded least one fall prey to them. It was hectic working in such an area alone at first, and he was assigned the duty of marking vehicles all day. There would be days when he had to drink beer all day to cope with the stress and sight of innocent people executed in broad day light.

He was gradually developing fervent desire for alcohol as a means of refuge to avoid such trauma of seeing innocent people slaughtered. In such an environment, the mind was completely in another world, and alcohol was the only remedy to address the situation. There were others who would prefer to smoke weed all day to calm their nerves, as the situation was chaotic with the sights of rebel soldiers with guns carrying rifles, including blood thirsty men who threatened your life for not submitting to their will and needed a short cut. But what was he supposed to do as a coding artist under the command of a career soldier? He had never held arms in his life and had no intention of holding one, but he needed to survive the war and take care of his family at home too. This was the only way to secure daily meals from the warehouse that rationed food for soldiers and civilians. His intention was to play it safe and survive this situation till the end by obeying orders and keeping in line with life.

Friends were made with so-called commandos, as they preferred to be called, and told them what they needed to hear, singing faint praises to gain recognition and be considered as one of theirs. It is hard to survive in an environment where people think differently and treat you as an outsider because you are not considered one of theirs. This is the point that so many of us go through daily by pretending to be another person when we are not. The Bible tells us another story of unique identity. We were created in the image and likeness of God.

So, God created mankind in his own image,
in the image of God he created them;
male and female he created them.
(Genesis 1:27)

Such is our identity, and it is so wonderful to know that we were created with a unique character. But if we go further into the reading, we will notice that the Lord looked after his creation and said that everything was beautiful. The Good Book speaks to us again, telling us how great we were created in the sight of God:

*So, God saw everything that he had
made, and behold, it was very
good. And the evening and the
morning were the sixth day.
(Gen.1:31)*

Childhood friends of Clarence were directly assigned to frontline rebel commanders and were seen riding the backs of pickup trucks heading to the war front and city center where government forces were located. There were others who longed to be like the rebels and got carried away by such fantasies. Their story had a sad ending as some were left behind as war casualties and later died on the battlefront, bodies unidentified. Clarence played it safe and decided to remain calm amidst this storm, building up his faith in God and trusting to see him through the end.

Gradually, he became known as the guy who placed numbers on cars, as most of the fighters were illiterate and could barely read and write. Therefore, those guys who joined forces with the rebels from the city had the edge over the rest of them. They would lead and teach them the way of life in the city center suburbs and even became commanders in certain areas within the city. Those living outside the rebel base area had different stories from those living within the conferment of his base areas. The area of Taylor Major compound, which later became Prince Johnson Base, was peaceful prior to the outbreak of the Liberian civil conflict. During the war, while under Johnson's control, avoiding the main roadway was advisable. The best decision was to take back routes to avoid the rebel leaders' convoy. Prince Johnson had a taste for good-looking light-colored women and would pick you up without question. Those were fearful days for men to have beautiful women as wives. Who would dare ask Johnson questions about taking his wife to spend days or nights with him?

Clarence knew a friend who got shot in the face by the rebel leader and survived the ordeal but was left deformed, while another woman was left for dead on a narrow road after encountering General Johnson. Gladly, they both survived with such scars to remember that while living in his controlled area, one had to be wise and do what would save the day. Clarence had no intention of running into him. He even remembers a time when he was assigned to his residence for a few days and was afraid the next morning upon hearing the news that a soldier keeping watch had mistakenly turned off the light switch and fallen asleep and was executed by Johnson. The next day, when his boss appeared at the general's residence, he pleaded with him to have his assignment changed. He went ahead and spoke with Johnson, highlighting his responsibilities at the motor pool with vehicle inventory and coding. He agreed, and Clarence was reassigned back to the motor pool with a sense of relief.

"It was a close call," Clarence said to himself and continued to perform his duties at the facility with workmates and friends that he had made. On less busy days, they would play games like chess, cards, and ludo also kept the gates closed until they heard cars pulling up for service. Suddenly, all games would be put away, and they returned and acted busy as though they were always at work. Who knew when Johnson or his assistant would arrive? No prior notices were given; they just showed up, and you must be prepared or face whatever came your way.

Fighting continued in parts of the besieged capital city, with government forces holding a portion of the city while Johnson's forces-maintained control of Bushrod Island, including the shipping port where food and other necessary supplies for survival were kept. A meeting was arranged at first, where the rebel leader visited President Doe at the military barracks and had a series of discussions about bringing the civil conflict to an end. This was deceptive in nature and reminded Clarence of the story of Samson and Delilah's love affair. From the lips of Delilah, one could sense deception and cunning, but Samson was so blindly in love to even sense deception with all that strength that he had. Such was the case of former President Doe giving his trust to the rebel leader Johnson, who tried to display support for someone he was desperate to slaughter for revenge. Doe allowed the rebel leader to depart in peace without a scratch. It seemed like they had not fully agreed on a way forward to peace, and Johnson returned to his Bushrod Island base as usual.

In the month of September, to be precise, on the ninth day, news came that the former president had been captured, and Clarence thought at first that this was a joke. Hearing gunfire and people rejoicing warranted his concern to look and see what was unfolding. There was news that President Doe's men were killed by Johnson's forces during a fierce exchange at the freeport of Monrovia. Clarence believed that this was an ambush, and Doe was set up by the ECOMOG and delivered to Prince Johnson.

Liz, a former British Broadcasting Corporation journalist, gave a detailed account of what had occurred, being present at the site of the incident and seeing it all. The president was shot, arrested, tied up, placed in the trunk of a car, and taken to Johnson's base in Caldwell for interrogation. It was in the afternoon when the residents of the community heard that the president had been arrested, and people began to gather to see a glance of a powerful and stubborn man. Some questions came to Clarence's mind, and he wondered why the president did not leave when, according to the news report, he had been given the offer to be flown to a safe place outside Liberia, but he later declined such an offer and decided to stand and fight to defend the oath of office he took as a leader. The future of every man is uncertain, as no one knows what tomorrow may bring. He was not the only leader to have fallen into the hands of his enemy. Even a powerful man like King Saul fell twice into the hands of David. In 1 Samuel 26:23, David said, "The LORD delivered you into my hand today, but I would not stretch out my hand against the LORD'S anointed."

When Clarence arrived, he saw the former president sitting on the ground with his hand tied behind his back, pleading for mercy while they had his ears cut off. There was a guy who had cut off something looking like a bead from around the former President's waist containing a small animal horn. Doe was seen from a distance being asked numerous questions, but the sight was awful, with blood running down the side of his face because of the cut. In anger, Clarence left the scene and wondered how great men fall so low and become vulnerable to society. There were many questions running through his head. Why did the former President cross the line knowing the reckless character of the rebel leader and his men, including the fact that he could not be trusted because of his arrogance?

The night was tense and had people afraid within the community while the rebel leader issued an alert and strict order. As a security measure, entrance to the base was prohibited, and residents should remain at home. He expected an attack from the government forces to rescue the president, the slain leader. Later that evening, the former president was pronounced dead at a clinic nearby due to maltreatment and blood clots from the inhumane way he was treated by the rebel leader and his men. His body was deposited at a local mortuary, where it was later removed after suspicion that an attempt to steal his body by his kinsman was in the making. The book of Genesis 9:6 tells us:

*"Whoso shredded man's blood, by
man shall his blood be shed:
for in the image of God made he man"*

Prince Johnson was such an unstable and unpredictable character, as noticed even by the peacekeeping force. He would agree to a discussion and, a moment afterward, had a change of mind, which was also dangerous to the peacekeepers' well-being and operation. How could one even trust such a leader with an unstable mind and be safe? Though it was the rebels who were in control of the shipping port and initiated welcoming the peacekeepers to the country, the city was besieged and under attack by another rebel group of men shielding rockets on the pier to prevent the landing of the peacekeepers. The leading rebel group considered the peacekeepers' occupational forces and prevented troops from running over the city capital.

Gen. Johnson had skills and was considered a master in guerrilla warfare, but his forces were short on a supply of arms and ammunition and badly depended on arms captured from fighting with government forces, including those supplies that were captured from the battlefield and fleeing soldiers. The rebel leader needed the peacekeepers to land and assist him in fighting his enemies off while also keeping government forces in check. It was a fierce battle, and innocent lives paid the price of a senseless war. Seeing mothers of infants die while the child was breastfeeding and others who felt sympathy taking the child off the dead mother's back was disheartening.

The food of the day was sugarcane, palm cabbage, palm kennel, and you could name it. People had to survive and turned to using creative improvisation methods for food to stay alive. There was assistance from foreign governments which was essential in delivering the supply of needed food and medication to the people of Liberia. Clarence recorded that the island was the only place to survive and had adequate food supplies. Prince Johnson fed the civilians with food, including his fighters, who fed extended family members also.

After President Doe's death at the hands of the rebel leader, tension began to ease, with the peacekeepers' actively trying to restore peace while Taylor remained unsatisfied and felt cheated that the peacekeepers had taken sides with INPFL forces. Clarence felt the same, being that Johnson was the first contact on the ground, and the peacekeepers were mostly inexperienced, apart from a few countries like Nigeria and Ghana, which headed the mission at first, being exposed to international peacekeeping duties.

The lives continued socially within a rebel-held territory, and they took a calculated risk too. It was on a nice Sunday afternoon while returning from the base; Clarence saw folks and family members gathered on the back porch of his house. Usually, the kids, including a familiar child soldier with a Beretta gun, would meet there and have fun. But this day was different and would change the family life forever. While playing, the child soldier mistakenly discharged his weapon and struck my cousin, who had just returned from church service and was still in her clothes.

Just in such time, another of Johnson's commandos, who originally made the fight from the beginning, passed by, saw the incident, and stopped. His first thought was to execute the child soldier in the presence of everyone. The child pleaded for his life but to no avail. Clarence was interested in his cousin getting medical attention, so they needed to take her to the clinic for a medic to see the child. During his absence, the commando soldier, called Rambo, shot and killed the child solder on the roadside leading to his house. Upon arrival at the clinic with his cousin, Edith was carried on the back of a family friend; we were asked what had occurred. Briefly, they explained to the nurse on duty, and he told them to wait for the specialist to come in. He had to leave. He left another older cousin to take care of Edith until the nurse arrived. At first, they were given the assurance that it was a minor issue, but with the soldier executing the child soldier, it became a major incident.

News had gotten to the general that the soldier had shot and killed the child soldier using his AK-47 rifle. He asked if the person shot had died because of the bullet. The reply was, "Not yet, but she was admitted to the clinic, receiving treatments." He, in return, said that should Clarence's cousin live, the soldier would be executed as an example for others to follow because the civilian was wounded and not dead, so there should be no reason for unnecessary killing. By morning, his cousin, who was shot in the abdomen, was pronounced dead. They knew that something sinister had taken place that night. With a strong fighter being threatened with execution in retaliation for wrongful execution, anything could happen to save his life. She was buried the following morning, wrapped in a cloth without a box, at the gravesite.

*****

The images of a civil conflict can be devastating and, at times, create a lasting impact on a person's life. Seeing all those acts of violence has created hatred and wounds that are almost impossible to heal. Perpetrators of those hideous crimes should be held accountable for inflicting such wounds on the masses. Not a moment goes by without Clarence experiencing some sort of flashback, trying to fight the psychological wounds within his mind. No medication can cure this illness, which was created by a group of angry men and women on a rampage, slaughtering fellow human beings.

Such was life in the war zone of Liberia. The untimely death of a child at the hands of another child soldier, among others, points to the danger of giving a child gun to carry, being untrained and inexperienced. The Bible points out that training children is the responsibility of every parent. But how can children be trained in such a time of uncertainty when the nation is at war with itself?

Train up a child in the way he should go and when he is old, he will not depart from it.
(Proverbs 22:6)

Our threat was not external but internal; we were at war with ourselves and did not even realize what damage would result after a decade of a senseless war. Power, greed, animosity, and weakness had caused us to go against one another. Where is the love as brothers and sisters which had been taught to us by our fallen folks? Our leaders became drunk and wicked from sleeping with the evil queen Jezebel and wanted power at all costs, ignoring the plight of the so-called masses. The result led us exactly to where we find our nation today with generations lost, trying to find identity in a forest of lost identity.

The plight of losing a child during this senseless war can never be forgotten and will take more than time to heal. The cold hands of death have snatched two of Clarence's children away through unknown illnesses and malnutrition. "We lost them," he cried and cursed the day he was born, realizing his plight was too much to bear. "How could one person be confronted with such pain and grief?" He asked. Why do we even have a God who remains quiet and lets His children go through terrible circumstances? We tend to pour out our grievances and emotions on God without realizing His plans for our lives. Despite these situations, our God always shows a smiling face behind every dark cloud of life. When faced with trials and tribulations, avoid complaining and seek the face of God, and the Father will reveal His plans for your life. The book of Jeremiah reminds us of this. He said:

"For I know the plans I have for you,"
declares the Lord, "plans to prosper
you and not to harm you, plans to give
you hope and a future"
(Jeremiah 29:11)

There is room for error when we do not wait on God's plan to get us out of our current situation and begin to judge God from a limited version of what He should be seen as. This is exactly where the enemies reside to launch the needed attack because of our limitation of God's purpose for our lives.

*****

The war had ceased, and the base was less busy with the presence of reduced soldiers. Soldiers secretly returned home, hoping to rebuild their lives, especially those living in the city of Monrovia. But some had been caught up in Monrovia and could not return to Nimba and the rest of the country because Taylor was still in control of greater Liberia. Returning could be a death sentence for some, while others would be labeled as traitors by their relatives.

This was a senseless war with brothers and sisters from biological parents fighting against one another. What sense did this make? But the end was far from that. One could only imagine what it would be like. Clarence remembered taking a trip on an ICRC contract to Taylor's rebel-held areas of Bomi County to deliver food. God is great as Clarence was afraid because the town had been under the control of the heartless commander of Charles Taylor known only as "Redd". There were stories of horror on how he executed pregnant women by opening their bellies and pulling out the unboned child, among other things. What if he identified him as the coding artist from the Prince Johnson area and got caught? He would be accused of being a spy. As God would have it, the food was delivered, and they were on their way home. Clarence held onto a rail in the back of the pickup truck, which was speeding, when a sudden bang in the road, because of potholes created by rockets launched during the war, took his grip off balance.

He was heading for death with his head crashing on the pavement from a moving car, and the driver was heading on. His

45

head was moving downward, and suddenly he felt a hand that pulled him up and placed his grip back on the rail of the truck. He felt something deep within as a chill ran down his spine, and he decided to sit in the car, thinking about what had just happened. He might have been chosen by God after going through all these unveiling situations, surviving near-death tragedies, and still alive. He remained quiet for the rest of the trip; even the guys at the back of the Kia pickup truck wondered about his silence.

"Are you okay?" They asked.

"Yes. Why?" He replied.

"You are so quiet," they said.

Deep within him, he knew that this was a miracle on how he survived, and those unseen but felt hands had delivered him from the evil hands of death. How could he consider himself a survivor or one who had to be chosen? If chosen, what could these reasons be, considering all he had been through? Or could this be regarded as an uncommon favor because he was sure that obeying the will of God was not the order of his day? Nevertheless, when they finally reached their destination Duala, Bushrod, everyone got out and headed back to Johnson's base. The commanding officer then asked, "Where are you guys from?" They lied that the car was in the repair shop all day, and we had to wait for it. There was nothing that he could do now that the war was coming to such an end, the peacekeepers were all around, and tension had cooled down.

While sitting at the motor pool, he was approached on a sunny day by the head of Johnson's ammo unit, who told Clarence that he had a job for him, but he would need two other persons to help. Clarence said, "Okay," and he took him to a 40-foot container guarded by two men holding rifles and told them to open it. They did, and to Clarence's surprise, it was filled with new green military helmets boxed up. He said that this was a secret mission. Johnson needed him to paint white on every one of those helmets, just like ECOMOG helmets look. Clarence told Commander John that they were going to need paint and spray guns, including thinner, to complete the job. They also needed food to feed his helpers and finish the job. In confidence, Clarence contacted two guys and told them the nature of the job and that he needed their commitment. Without any hesitation, the guys accepted, and when the supplies were given, the job began, and they worked until the entire container of helmets was coated with white spray paint.

Clarence began to wonder why Johnson instructed him to spray-paint those helmets just like ECOMOG when the war was closing, and the forces did not need the helmets. The meaning of the assignment finally came through when he was informed that it was a mission, and being the person who completed it, he had to be eliminated before the news went out. Upon receiving the message, he hurriedly picked up a few things and began to head out of the area. Luckily, he took his father with him and asked him to carry his bag. Upon reaching the Iron Gate, the guard told him that he was not permitted to leave on Johnson's order. He knew as a point of survival, something had to be done right away because his father was able to leave him behind. He asked for the commanding officer and asked, "Do you know me?"

The officer replied, "Yes, from the motor pool." Clarence said that Johnson had asked him to do a favor at the Stockton Creek Bridge, and should he resist, upon Johnson's return, it would be his head that would roll. After a while, the officer allowed him to go and took him aside, saying, "You must hurry and be back." That was the last time, and he breathed a sigh of total relief when he caught up with his dad, who asked him not to return. Johnson accused the interim president of trying to rip the country off by printing new bank currencies for the country without giving the total number of what was printed. A lot was going on, and trust was no longer among the forces, the Interim Government National Unity and the rebel forces. Taylor and Johnson withdrew their representatives from the power-sharing government of national unity. Johnson asked his representatives to return to the base, but others refused to return and remained in the government. Anyone would think something was in the making, but neither Taylor nor Johnson could be trusted. Johnson was unpredictable and could flip at any time. The worst was yet to come for residents living in the city of Monrovia, considered a haven from Taylor. ECOMOG and the world had invested resources in the Liberian civil conflict, including numerous and costly peace conferences.

Chapter 3
FIGHT FOR SURVIVAL

It was during the confidence visit established by ECOMOG that the rebels began another plan. Taylor wanted to be president, and that could only happen if he captured Monrovia and got rid of the peacekeeping group ECOMOG, which prevented him from running over the city. Plan of confidence visits gave both rebel forces the time to reunite as fighters were getting weary and needed to return and begin a normal life. Clarence explained that both Prince's INPFL and Taylor's NPFL decided on a plan to reunite and bury the differences, but Johnson was betrayed by his soldier serving as negotiators, including his next-in-command, Varney, who switched allegiance to Charles Taylor's forces.

A week had passed since Clarence left the base, and his girlfriend requested to visit his folks for the weekend but never made it back, and he consented to a decision that was regrettable till today. She was captured together with his parents and taken to another area, hours away, for a month as a human shield. A friend of his was a journalist gave him the hookup employed at a government ministry with the interim government, in the division that oversaw government drawings and projects.

The rebels launched Operation Octopus that night in the month of October in the city of Monrovia and the environs; it was horrible. Residents of the city were in disarray as rockets and rocket-propelled grenades were seen landing in the city of Monrovia. It became known that the helmets printed were meant for the rebel forces to penetrate under the disguise of a peacekeeper. For a minute, there was confusion, and rebels had been planted within city limits with instructions to attack from within. They had fundamental problem as they were deployed and did not know the city of Monrovia and were apprehended or killed by ECOMOG forces in action. On the other hand, Johnson used displace rescued children as a human shield by operating a child center and got out with the help of the peacekeepers and the United Nations, taking the children out of harm's way.

His second-in-command had turned against him, most of his loyal fighters had switched sides, and his position was compromised. His gun firing pins were taken out when he came to realize most of his fighters were killed while others joined NPFL to advance on Monrovia. Clarence could not sleep and began to feel guilty. Why did he let the family go to his parents? Another moment of horror was about to be experienced by the family. Here he was again, escaping another tragedy unharmed. Was this a pattern of reoccurrences, or just that the favor of God was on his life, taking him through these terrible situations? He was so afraid that the thought of committing suicide came to his head. He would rather take his own life than be taken and executed by rebel forces should they overrun the city and find him alive. Nights passed, and they saw the emergence of a new fighting group trained by the interim government known as the Black Berets. There were various warring factions formed against Taylor's decision to forcibly take over the capital city. One group was known as ULIMO-K, which later broke up to form ULIMO-J and LPC, among other things. Every group had guns and committed atrocities across the country. They all had one thing in common: Taylor must go, which was almost impossible. The real reasons for organizing these factions were to secure a seat at the table of the unity conference in forming a power-sharing government. It is evil when you realize how men of war will plan and use humans to satisfy personal greed in the name of unity, pretending to seek the welfare of the people they abused.

The fighting finally ended in Monrovia as Johnson was taken out of the process of elimination and given asylum in Nigeria. The rest of the warring factions decided to keep the pressure on Taylor. ECOMOG maintained control of security together with the local security apparatus in Monrovia and its environs. But there was another problem with the ECOMOG peacekeepers. They launched a reprisal on Liberian civilians during the aftermath of Operation Octopus, including intimidation, harassment, and even summary executions. Clarence recalled sitting on his front porch alone with a few other family members, playing the game of check-up when an ECOMOG truck pulled up with armed soldiers and asked if they saw a group of guys who had earlier broken into a store and made away with goods. To the soldiers' dismay, they said they were not aware of anything.

They pulled their guns at Clarence and two other guys, instructing them to get into the car, and they could not refuse under gunpoint. They were taken to the grounds of the Executive Mansion and severely flogged till dawn after useless interrogations. Clarence grew mad and wanted to resist, but another soldier advised him to stay calm as the other officer would not hesitate to shoot him dead. "They have done it before," the officer stated, "and trust me, he will kill you if you resist." Clarence took his advice and remained calm as the other soldier brutally flogged them till blood was running out of their flesh. At this point, what could he say? Was God still around and listening to his cry for help? Later during the early morning hours, they were taken to an ECOMOG checkpoint and dropped off on the Capital Bypass.

A family member had come to visit Clarence, and being a journalist, he heard the news, saw the bruises, and decided to take him to meet his buddy at a local daily office. There, they met a renowned journalist, and he reported the story in the daily. He received no apologies from the peacekeepers and could only imagine how many others had suffered a similar ordeal, even death, at the hands of the peacekeepers. After all these incidents, an offer came that Clarence could not resist. The question was: "Do you want to travel out of Liberia"? "Of course," he replied because he had no other option but to run away. Anywhere would be great to escape the men of the night who fed on human blood for wine.

People were leaving the country for fear of more bloodshed, intimidation, and hunger. Clarence accepted the gesture to leave. There was random abuse of power, and those in authority had limited control. It was a country deeply at war and trying to calm a situation that they had no experience with. In other words, it was a period of trial and error.

The civil conflict indeed brought sorrow upon many people and created emotional scars within their hearts, wounds that would - never be healed nor forgotten. Clarence's kids were lost during the conflict, and he often thinks of how beautiful they could have turned out had they been alive. The world is such a crazy place and gets cruel at times, depending on the situation that life may bring. It is a beautiful and colorful world, yet people still get lost and must struggle to find their way home at times. His eyes have witnessed authorities, and scars left on his body bears witness to what hardship is like. Experiencing murder and physical abuse by those entrusted to keep you safe speaks volumes. Guess they say it is survival of the fittest, and to survive the ordeal, one must be mentally disciplined by bearing with pain.

.

Chapter 4
WRONG PLACE, WRONG TIME

He met a lady, and they became friends. She would visit him every evening after work, and they would walk and talk along the beach trying to take his feeling of isolation away. Gradually, he felt a release from the pain of feeling lost and deserted in his country of birth. Things seemed like they were falling into place, and Clarence decided that he would invest in a business center and begin a new life upon his return. Everything going according to plan. One thing was missing: the finance to start a business. "Where will the funding come from?" he asked.? He had been down this route and learned not to worry about things beyond his control.

One night, he recalled, he headed home and fell asleep after drinking at a local bar. The use of alcohol regularly can lead a person into addiction, thus becoming an alcoholic. He did not seem like an alcoholic. He carried himself well within every community, even after occasionally taking in a few drinks. But this was about to change. In the early morning, he woke up, still feeling tired from the previous night. While lying across the bed of his friend's room, he had an attack.

Feeling unpleasant in his left arm, he noticed that his mouth began to twist to the left of his face. A voice said to him lift your arms to pull your mouth back into position. He obeyed and shouted, "Jesus! Jesus! Jesus!" as he tried to shift his face back into position as usual. It was difficult at first, so he tried the use of both hands, and he was successful that his face took shape again. But it was too late as he had wet the bed of a stranger, like a child in his mother's bed. He sat there feeling ashamed and embarrassed. It is shameful for a man to wet a lady's bed: he felt guilty as she had gone to prepare breakfast that morning. He hurriedly got up and took the sheets from the bed to be washed. Just in time, she returned to the room and asked, "Why are you changing the sheets?"

"They're dirty," he replied.

"No, I just changed them yesterday," she said.

He narrated what took place, and the look on her face was strange as she shouted, "What?"

"What would she think of me?" He narrated, "She Probably thought I was a foolish guy."

The lady left and returned to the room. She saw his facial expression, then asked, "Are you ok?"

He replied that he was okay but later said he was not. Still astonished, he replied that it was a stroke. "You should first thank

God, and try to see the doctor, as the situation could have changed, and I would have been in big trouble," she said. But Clarence did go; instead, he spent the rest of his day thinking about what had happened.

He was indeed in the wrong place and at the wrong time. What could he have said to his wife and family for being so careless? What would the lady have explained if the worst happened in her home? These are calculated risks that men do for the lust of the flesh. Consuming alcohol and drugs will make you vulnerable to tragedies. Being a married person and having sex outside of marriage is a sin. Not only that, but it also invites unwanted forces into your home and places our families at risk. Whenever we engage in the act of cheating on our spouse, there is a level of disrespect for that person. Spiritually, the Bible tells us that we should not be unequally yoked. By sharing the bed of another person who is not your spouse, you might be entering into a soul covenant with the devil. After a night of pleasure, you depart, unaware that you have deposited unwanted illness or monitoring agents within what was supposed to be God's temple. And as time progresses, we notice changes within our homes, like disputes without resolution, illness, and even death. The father or mother has invited enemies, chaos, and confusion within the home.

Just for a night of enjoyable time, Clarence nearly lost his life in another woman's bed. This body that God has given us was meant to be the temple of the Holy Spirit:

*"What? know ye not that your body is the
temple of the Holy Ghost which is in you, which
ye have of God, and ye are not your own?"*
(1 Corinthians 6:19)

When we pollute the temple, our body is left with no place for the Holy Spirit to reside. If the spirit leaves us, we will not have guidance and protection, which leaves us as easy prey for the devil.

Despite these changes that we go through in our lives, God has never left us and gone too far. He gives us the option to make choices and, at times, even decisions regarding which path to take in life. The freedom of choice given unto us will then lead us into destruction, begging for mercy and forgiveness.

"This was a stroke," he said, "but it had been reversed." "What could he have said, being in the wrong place and at the wrong time?" He wondered. Not many folks go through a stroke like that and walk away without the intervention of a medical practitioner as though nothing had occurred. This was not at work because he was in the wrong place and opted not to be there at all. But for the grace of God, he had been saved again by the hands that healed, and it was a miraculous miracle in Clarence's life. His previous situation will create a lifetime memory, and he had another thing to add to his list of what God has done for him. One thing he remembered, and it was true that the wages of sin is death.

"For the wages of sin is death:
but the gift of God is eternal life through
Jesus Christ our Lord"
(Romans 6:23)

But it doesn't stop there and goes on to say that we are not going to die prematurely if we surrender to the will of God. It is not the will of God our Father to see any one of His children perish, but we should seek redemption through His son, Jesus Christ.

The gift of life is a precious and undeserved gift from God. As the creator, He has absolute authority to decide who lives and to whom He is going to show mercy. For Clarence, this was love and mercies beyond favor. He had been saved repeatly, so this must be a sound that God was about to take him to another level of his life. In the following week, what occurred in his life was amazing as he watched the hands of God working wonders in his life.

Clarence has been battling demons for years, from early childhood to adulthood, yet he remains defiant and stubborn. God loves us so much and is waiting for us to willingly return to His arms of love. Due to his behavior, he went through moments of pain and sorrow, yet he remains determined to survive. With all he did, he never relinquished his faith in God and kept on trusting and believing. At times, we will go through situations and trials meant to evaluate our faith in God. The decision that Clarence made was foolish and could have cost his life or caused some other physical harm, yet he was saved by the hands of God. It was all part of God's plan that would lead to his conviction and later testimony as he was going through stages of preparation to serve. We allowed this body of ours to go through emotional disorder and face needless pain due to disobedience. "Wouldn't this world be a beautiful place if we could just obey God and live according to His plans for our lives?" He asked. God's plan for us is to propose and not to harm us, as declared in the book of Jeremiah 29:11.

"For I know the plans I have for you,"
declares the Lord, "plans to prosper you
and not to harm you, plans to give you
hope and a future."

He has been taken through trials, failures, and successes in a world of uncertainty but remains unhappy. Clarence was still lost and trying to find his way back home to where he needed to be, but he could not see the light. Whenever we become so comfortable spending time with the devil, he creates an impression that we cannot live without doing what isn't right. But the Bible also tells us that the Lord is our strong tower in times of trouble and trials. It is important to keep in mind that not all trials and situations come to end our lives. There are times when these things will make us even stronger in our faith. Clarence was going in a circle like the children of Israel in the wilderness that lasted 40 years. The journey should have been shorter, but disobedience to God kept them in the wilderness, and the presence of God was with them.

Clarence had lived in another country for over a decade and learned the culture of the people, including survival skills. He had faith, and it was due to that trust in God that kept him grounded during all those trials: he never gave up. He had good days and bad days too. "It is important to say that during both days, God was with me and never left my side," he said. "I felt His presence at times and knew that He was there but could not realize His fullness living in sins, yet He was with me. Why was he there for me when I did not listen to His voice and could not see living in sins, which kept me in the dark? Living in the dark is painful and filled with unknown demons and deceptions." It was those lies that kept Clarence living in a state of denial and having the presence of godliness but denying it.

The following night came, and while sleeping, Clarence saw a revelation from the Lord, giving him a white envelope. He woke up early the next morning and told folks what he had seen in his dream. Nobody knew what to say, but he was sure that something was about to happen that would change his life. Within two days, he received a call from his wife, the long-awaited call. It has taken him over ten years waiting on God's time, and it was now time for God to speak. When it comes to God, numbers do not matter in His sight, for He makes everything beautiful in His own time. The call said that

Clarence had an appointment with the US embassy. He was dumbfounded at first and thought it was a trick. He spoke to God and made a request, asking for a sign to move forward. He had been burnt so many times, tricked, even duped, all in the name of seeking greener pastures. He had not given up on God and knew that in God's time, everything would be beautiful. "I'm tired trying," said Clarence, "and just need to rest now." Later that night, as he slept, he spoke to God while in his corner and said, "If this is really you, then I need the interviewer at the embassy to ask me three questions only as a sign of your presence."

Faith is the key to the solution of doubts and fears in every believer's quest for success. He spoke to God as David said,

"I sought the Lord, and he heard me, and
delivered me from all my fears.
They looked unto him and were lightened and
their faces were not ashamed"
(Psalm 34:4-5)

He had been trying all his life, never given up, and still trusted that God could deliver as promised but had a fear of falling again. "This is what we go through at times," he said. "We pray, fast, and even sing the Lord's song but remain in doubt because of our fear. This is just the place where the enemies meant for us to be living in doubt and darkness. The enemies will keep us in this place of spiritual isolation to use us. We have a God that is far greater than our fear, but we still choose to live with the devil and allow him to keep us as slaves when salvation is free."

Clarence went on to attend his interview, and as he had requested, though in doubt, he decided to try God. He was ushered into the office and took a seat, still praying with little faith. He remembered the sight of an elderly man who greeted him and asked, "Who's filing for you?"

He replied, "my wife."

"What's her name?"

"MaryAnn," he said.

The interviewer asked him to step outside the office. At first, it was fun. When he came out of the office, others looked at him in astonishment. "What happened?" A lady asked.

"Why," he asked.

"Because you are the fastest person to have stepped out of that office."

He joked and replied, "I was denied again."

Reality began to sink into Clarence's head. God was fulfilling His words saying to him in a tiny voice, "This is your season of fulfillment." After all the process had gone through, Clarence was given a visa to travel overseas. He was glad and headed to an upscale restaurant to celebrate with a one-man party. There, he ate and had some drinks till he was filled before calling his wife to narrate what had taken place and that he was finally on his way to join her. God had delivered as promised, but Clarence did not make a commitment to serve the God of the angel's army.

Chapter 5
THE FALL

It was on one working day of the week; Clarence couldn't remember the month, but he knew it was in the winter season. His wife was pregnant, and he had set off for work with the promise of coming back. Before I go on, let me state an observation, he narrated how important it is to seek God's guidance every day prior to heading out from home. He made such a mistake, and it nearly took away his life in 2006. At the office, it was a usual morning meeting, and after taking hold of his daily assignment and keys to his assigned truck, he set off.

He worked as a field technician and headed out to complete a customer requisition. It was his first job of the fateful morning under freezing weather. He arrived, greeted the customer, and asked about the issue faced by the customer. A swimming pool outside the customer's residence was filled with frozen water. He worked inside the house and needed to fix something on top of the roof of the customer's home. The customer asked:

"Aren't you cold?" He replied, "Yes, I am, but what can I do? This is part of the job, working in inclement weather." Clarence needed a ladder to access the roof. He went on to his assigned truck to pull down a ladder and put it up against the house. The Lord has fulfilled His promise by taking him through every dark cloud and the near-death situations in life, but he was yet to surrender in obedience to God's will. He had climbed the ladder; before reaching the top, a loud bang was heard.

Clarence had fallen twenty feet from the roof unto the pavement, with his head nearly hitting the ground. He tried to use his right hand as a cushion, but due to the nature of the fall, and the weight associated with it, he could not hold on for long. "I saw stars falling when my head hit the pavement," He said. What he did not realize was that he was unconscious from the fall. Upon gaining consciousness, he awoke and began to move, which was wrong. He felt his head, checking for the sight of blood, but there was none. Neither did he know that his right hand was fractured. Hurriedly, he got up and began to move but was stopped in his track by the customer.

"Are you ok?" he asked.

"Sure, I am," he replied.

"Are you sure? Should I call the ambulance?" he asked.

Clarence replied, "Nope."

The customer had an idea about the incident but could not prevail on Clarence's freedom to leave and head back to his office, promising that another person would be sent to complete the job. His refusal to call the paramedic would have caused him to lose his right arm. Within minutes, his arm had swollen, and reality began to set in. Prior to leaving the customer's premises, he radioed his boss, explaining that he got wounded.

His boss asked, "Can you drive to the office?"

He replied, "Yes."

"Are you sure?"

"Yes," he replied again.

While driving, his right hand began to swell. He was rushed to the local emergency center for diagnosis and treatment. After examination, it was discovered that both his right arm and spine were affected by the fall. "I could have been dead by then," he stated, "but for the saving grace of the highest God, I survived." God remains our stronghold in times of trial and unseen situations; He led us through this path that we cannot see at first. But in the end, when we deeply reflect on our past, His hands are always there to save a falling soul and keep him from destruction. Clarence said, "God has no season and cares less about our timing in life. He controls the timing, and situations also set the pace for success but within His perfect timing.

The good old book tells us that the righteous shall inherit the earth and that only true believers shall see God. Clarence has not been obedient nor perfect in living to the will of God, but his faith in God has never wavered. No matter what the situation might be, Clarence keeps his faith. "I was not born of a rich family," he said, "but my parents taught me Christian and moral values to live by. Life has its set of rules that humans should live by to be successful and at peace with one another. But God has given us His plan for our lives, and that is to prosper and not fail. So we wonder and begin asking why bad things happen to good folks. Our ways are not the ways of God, nor can our thoughts be compared to that of God. Things that seem so bad and terrible to you might be part of God's plan for your life. When I am confused and unsatisfied with temptations and trials in my life, I retire to a quiet room and speak to God like a friend. We have nice conversations, and he tells me his plan, and I'm relieved from my struggles because God has spoken to me."

The doctors at the ER could not attend to Clarence's situation and referred him to a specialist. He got concerned, and fear began to sink within his spirit. "What has happened to me, and is it that serious, Lord? Will my hands function as before, such as lifting and holding his newly born child?" The specialist diagnosis showed that Clarence had suffered from post-concussion syndrome. He could barely record what had taken place at the time of the fall. Second, the specialist stated that he needed surgery on his right hand to ease the swelling of tissues. The surgery was scheduled for three weeks and was performed. Healing was gradual, but it helped ease the pain, and Clarence had one concern.

With his spine being twisted, he needed to see another specialist. The doctor was bold and told him that he also needed surgery but that his case was crucial and needed a spine conference prior to making the final decision. "God," he said, "are you listening? And if you are listening to what the doctors are saying, what is your will for this? I do not want another surgery, Lord, not a spinal surgery." He begged. When you have been through trials and hardships, including betrayals in life, you form this alliance with a person who will always be there for you and understands every situation that is going wrong. At this point, Clarence turned to God for consolation believing what God said that life and death lie on our tongues, and we should just speak the word:

"Death and life are in the power of the tongue.
And those who love it will eat its fruit"
(Proverbs 18:21)

Every word that comes out of our mouths as humans is transformed into a spirit. Be careful what comes out of your mouth, and be wise to think twice before making statements. Refrain from making commitments when you are angry or emotional, as it has the tendency to hurt you later. The spine conference ended, and the doctor said they decided that the surgery would be a high risk for Clarence.

"Do you still feel that much pain?" he asked him.

Clarence replied, "Yes." And said to the doctor, "I do not need the surgery anymore."

"Why?" the doctor asked.

"Because God is going to heal me, and I can live with my pain while I wait," he replied.

The doctor called the case worker aside and had a discussion with her for a while. She returned to Clarence and asked him again. "What happened? The doctor just informed me that you refused the surgery." He said, "That's right. I consulted God, and He told me that I should not have back surgery and he's going to heal me." This is where we take authority as children of God and speak life within our situation. God has spoken to you in private now speak to the circumstance in public. Don't expect doctors and nurses to understand your level of communication with God. In fact, only a few will understand what you are speaking about. You're given authority by God that is higher than theirs. God is the spiritual doctor, and they are the physical doctors. Clarence depended on a spiritual doctor who could provide permanent healing without restriction. He listened and obeyed the doctor's order as required but still trusted God to do the rest.

Clarence took his medications and had a shot inserted into his lower spine. "A yearly prescription," said the doctor, "No heavy lifting and no horseplay." He obeyed and left the hospital with a smile because he knew God had spoken, and he did not doubt but proclaimed healing and moved on. "It has been thirteen years now," he shouted, "and I have never taken a single shot in my back and never had pains."

What a mighty God we serve. We should walk in faith and not fear and believe in the resurrection of Jesus Christ and the power given unto us. Though we may fall at times, there is always hope of a comeback through faith. There's a difference between believers and those that do not believe in Christ's resurrection. To the believer, principalities and power were destroyed while hope and faith were given to walk in.

Chapter 6
REFUGEE LIFE

The promise of a prosperous or better way of life must always be received with optimism but, at the same time, be open to renewing opportunities. When circumstances occur, always have a backup plan or alternatives. After a while, the opportunity came to travel to a neighboring country Ghana, and Clarence was delighted and even went to the freeport of Monrovia to board the ship. However, he was afraid to board the ship after seeing the amount of water discharged from the ship. Like a story told by a sea fearer, he decided to use his skills and get a plane ticket. He went to a ticket agent and negotiated a deal with him, giving him the amount that he had, which was less than the ticket price. In return, the agent needed a business card printed for him, so he did the job and got a one-way ticket to Accra, Ghana, on an Air Ivoire flight. After hours of flying, he finally arrived in Ghana and presented his travel document (laissez-passer) to the immigration officer, who granted him entry.

He was given a number for the location of the residence where his girlfriend's family resided. Unfortunately for him, the phone lines were out, and the matter got worse because there was no physical address in the area. How do you find a way out in a strange land with folks speaking strange languages that you cannot understand? Did he leave Liberia to get lost in a country that he would later lean to, which has strong traditional beliefs and foreign gods?

He arrived with a hundred United States dollars in his pocket from Liberia. The currency used in Ghana was the cedis, and the conversion rate was strange to him. This was his first trip outside Liberia, and the local languages of Ghanaians were strange to him. In Liberia, they lived around Ghanaians and were friends with them too. He often heard them speak in local languages if they did not want you to understand their conversation.

He boarded a taxi to an unknown area where the driver was supposed to find him at a Liberian gathering to locate his family. Knowing that he had the cash, the driver instead drove him around and charged him an unspecified amount for no reason. His arrival time at Kotoka International Airport was around 3:30 p.m. local time. The drivers who took a turn on him would take him to another place and hand him to other drivers, charging him for every ride, knowing that he was lost. They decided to capitalize on his ignorance by earning their daily wages.

He was hungry, tired, and just needed sleep, but where would he sleep, having no idea about the cost of a hotel or another place to rest? Finally, after eight exhausting hours of riding around, he found a driver who agreed to take him to the Liberian Camp for the remaining amount of cash in his hand, which was thirty USD. The driver insisted that Clarence would be able to find his folks thereafter; he explained to him that it was his last cash on hand. Being so exhausted, he had to agree to his request, and they headed in the direction of the camp, which was a thirty-minute drive. Upon reaching the refugee camp, the driver woke him up as he had fallen asleep during the ride after such a long day. He said, "This is where your people reside. Just ask someone. I am sure they might know your relatives." There were tents erected by the United Nations for refugees, and walking through, God did send me someone who knew him very well. Upon arrival, he was recognized by Archibald, who spoke to him and explained the ordeal he had suffered to him.

He said that he could remember seeing other family members around there, but they would not be able to find them till morning, and he could spend the night with him there. Clarence gladly agreed to finally have some rest and peace of mind. The next morning, he went out and played basketball after being woken up by the heat of the sun. Ghana is a country where the sunrise is early in the morning and will wake you up. He was able to find the guy later in the morning and thanked him, bidding him farewell. The refugee camp was a vast land that had been identified by the government of Ghana through the leadership of President Rawlings as a courtesy. It was a great gesture for the people of Liberia, who had fled the war and were seeking temporary refuge until the war came to an end.

After a few days, the news got to the family that he had arrived and was at the camp. They decided to find him and, after a few weeks, they decided to relocate to Accra to live as one family. The camp became Clarence's home, and it was difficult to survive in another man's country which spoke a foreign language. Ghana speaks several languages, depending on the region in which you reside. In Accra, for instance, they spoke the local languages. The hospitality was great at first when Clarence's family newly arrived and were tasked to find a place and build a house that would serve as the family home. They needed building materials, to begin with, for a home with many family members, including kids.

Little did they know that this would be their home for the next decade because the power, greed, and selfishness of the warring factions in Liberia would seize every opportunity to make Liberians suffer to enrich themselves. There were peace conferences, one after another, with little or no positive results. Clarence recalled that there was a time when the president, as the chairman of ECOWAS, was weary of deadlock in peace conferences and insisted that no one leave the conference hall till a peace agreement was reached. He stated that civilians were dying, and the cost of peacekeeping operations was hurting the regional body's resources.

Families based in the United States were their main source of survival, as they would send remittances regularly to cater to the families in Ghana. Through the help of that, people were able to purchase cement, zinc, and blocks and even pay construction workers. Life was not a ride to survive in the camp, even with the help of the United Nations, which provided monthly food ration supplies, among other basic essential commodities. The source of water was another problem. Ghana is like a savanna; water has been a problem for decades because of the constant hot and humid weather. They must dig into the earth and wait for hours, sometimes till early morning, when they need to do laundry for the kids. The source of drinking water was either tankers supplying water through the camp management or private water reservoirs constructed by Liberians who purchased and sold water to others at discounted prices for their source of income.

Their only source was remittance from the United States through family members or friends. Clarence had no relative in the US to depend on. Besides God, his creative mind and hands were the only means of survival. But he had a child and a mother to cater to, and survival was important to him. How could he find a means of generating income to care for the family when even the locals were finding it difficult to obtain jobs within Accra? There were men on the camp who had to perform manual labor by creating bricks from the earth and selling them to others as a source of income, while others had to learn skills such as carpentry, masonry, crocheting, sewing, tie, dye, and batik from the center established through the International Rescue Committee Skills Training Center.

Creating the center was important for Liberians to learn meaningful skills to survive and become competitive while living as refugees and upon returning to Liberia when the civil conflict was over. Not everyone had the opportunity to attend such a training center, as others were illiterate and had to cater to their families. How do you survive in such a hostile climate without being creative and thinking outside the box?

Some mothers and fathers had to sell merchandise daily in the market to cater to the family and Childs' educational needs. A public high school was built to educate the kids on the camp, but the parents had to purchase necessities: copybooks, pencils, pens, uniforms, and even lunch. Survival was the key, giving rise to the creation of criminal activities as well. Some females had to get involved in one of the oldest known social professions as a means of livelihood by going to the city at night and performing acts. Hustling was the order of the day. Males resorted to games of all sorts, even creating things that didn't exist just to survive. But in all, it is fair to say that despite those terrible times, God was still merciful and good to them.

Fear thou not; for I am with thee: be not dismayed;
for I am thy God: I will strengthen thee; yea,
I will help thee; yea, I will uphold thee
with the right hand of my righteousness.
(Isaiah 41:10)

There were churches of every denomination, and Sunday was busy indeed, like a fashion exhibit. You could see folks beautifully dressed up heading to church services. After service, the afternoon was climaxed by gathering at various places of entertainment to drink and have fun. Such was a time for gathering and hustling to meet friends who could afford and ask for financial assistance also for the coming week. Folks looked up to meeting others on Sunday because it was the time; if all goes well, you will have something to depend on to begin the week and provide for your family.

Such gatherings were also a point where people engaged in the sale of goods and services by engaging in lots of activities. We called it connections, and Clarence witnessed the sale and consumption of drugs by young men. He witnessed others consume their last penny and even had to leave personal belongings such as expensive watches, clothing, shoes, and the like, to compensate for drug consumption charges in some ghetto.

You may be wondering how he could see what was taking place and not get involved in the activities. He was not an angel either, but he could assure you that neither did he participate in the sale of drugs nor consume any. Times were extremely tough on the camp, especially when he arrived and did not have a place to lay his head but stayed with others in a packed room. The sneaker he wore from Liberia was green and white in color, and he had one traveling bag of clothes. Those sneakers were worn until they burst on his feet, and his pants were also faded because of frequent washing and were later torn. He had to do laundry, purchase breakfast, and eat a meal, and he needed cash or some assistance. The remittance from family members was insufficient, but it did help, especially with taking care of the kids.

His family was large, and being the humble one, the kids' laundry was no easy task. Done on Saturday, it took the entire morning as five kids played in the dirt too. Yes, indeed, souls were sold to the devil for ransom to satisfy their hungry stomachs and to feed loved ones and family. They engaged in a trade that involved looted national treasures. Little did they know that the sale of those looted national treasures would harm them in one way or another. Clarence stated he rubbed shoulders with corrupt law enforcement officers, and the sky became his limit. Money was no problem as it came in every currency in the world. There was no fixed price on the street hustle. Operating in a fast lane involved finding a client and, if successful, naming your price, and the client would pay cash, and the job was performed. There would be no return as goods, once purchased, could not be returned either, so it was a win-win business.

Do not get me wrong; this venture was risky at times, and being arrested by the authorities whose aim was to eradicate the business and limit the fraud. Because of Clarence's connections in the agency, he would get constant updates on upcoming raids and operation areas to avoid. In a tough world like theirs, information always came in handy when you pay for it. There were higher-ups involved in this business; many middlemen made it difficult even to know the boss. To become a leader in such a trade, you must be willing to extend your territory. You must break the rules, make enemies and strange friends for a moment, and then reconcile after the deal is done. Nothing is personal, just that the business underworld can sometimes be so cruel.

He was introduced to many people in this business and had lunch with them on numerous occasions, especially when he needed help or consultation. People traded in illicit money cards and would easily purchase tickets at a discounted price for cash upfront payment. He never asked where those cards came from and did not handle the cards but had to deal with a contact who probably never knew the main source. Sometimes, he had to disguise himself and dress like one of the locals to penetrate and get what he needed in no-go areas at odd hours of the night. The ghettos were great and the source of relative information, and you would be surprised by the personalities that showed up after hours.

There were times when traveling for eight hours both ways would be necessary to perform the task and get the cash as he took risks and was so brave at the time. Through this, he remained a very generous person and would assist single moms, widows, and kids in need of assistance. There was no day when he would wake up in the morning and not receive a guest asking for assistance at his door or even take a walk without someone asking for help. But that was the way of the refugee camp; people needed help and could not afford a meal or necessities for the upkeep of their kids. You would go through all these hustles daily and return home, sometimes late at night, only to see someone who needed urgent assistance. How could you just move on without lending a helping hand to those who needed a daily meal? There were kids who needed to be in school the next day or purchase water to take a shower and had no money. Grandparents took custody of kids fleeing the civil conflict, leaving parents behind. This was the world in which they lived, and they had to stand up for others at a time when they had nobody to speak up for them. They bonded as refugees and maintained such bonds with most by linking on social media and reminiscing about their years of struggle for survival. Friends and relatives were left behind in an area called Z, meaning "the end," as stated in the English alphabet, for a lost relative who never saw the promised land (America or Europe).

Clarence was recommended to a visiting client from another country who needed his services. They spoke about the price, and the client agreed to pay. He made an advance deposit but never said the rest of the cash was in another country. In the middle of a deal, you cannot back off it's too dangerous for both parties. They called it an "Alarm," and it was the last place Clarence intended to be. He was running out of options and asked the client who would pay for the transportation. Clarence was shaken and had second thoughts about the trip, including the security at the borders when crossing. If caught with the merchandise, he could face jail time. But that was nowhere near what he was about to face. After hours of traveling, they finally made it to the borders, and it was dark. The client told Clarence to follow him into the dark. Clarence was speechless. "Why?" he asked. The client made him understand that they had to bypass the border through the dark river. The client spoke French with the canoe operator and gave him a fee. There was a silence mixed with fear and regrets. Why did he leave his family, he wondered. Frightened, they boarded the canoe to the other side. In the middle of the dark river, the operator explained that many lives had been lost there in the water. He felt cold and asked for God's protection to carry them to the other side. And He did hear his prayers as they landed on the border of Ivory Coast. Upon landing, the border guards had been notified of people by-passing, so they began speaking some French, and they were able to get through, but the folks behind them got caught and were taken to jail. After that, they took a twelve-hour chartered taxi from the border to Abidjan and were stopped by security forces along their way, bribing their way through after giving the merchandise to the vehicle's driver for safekeeping. Almost reaching their destination, they were pulled over by a security officer who asked for their travel documents. When they presented them, he wondered why they did not have arrival stamps within the passports. They tried to bribe him, but he resisted, saying that the offered amount was little. After hours of negotiations, he released them. He was terrified again but glad that they were there.

Another thing that was going through Clarence's mind was whether this client was reliable and what would happen if he failed to fulfill his promise. How was he going to make the journey back? But it was late, and the client gave him a room to spend the night, but he was only praying for dawn to head back. Once he had the cash, he could find his way back. That morning, he awoke only to discover that his apartment was filled with females, all waiting to be transported to Europe. The agent had instructed them to prepare breakfast for him, and they did. He had to wait till noon to receive the money transfer from Europe. It came through, and he delivered as promised. He took him to a bus station, where he took a taxi to the border, and it was easier than the previous night's journey. Finally, he got through the border and headed home after a terrible night. God had covered him again.

Clarence kept his faith in God, and there were times when he tried to seek other gods, but to no avail. Those fetish priests are all liars and con artists; they would tell you something, and you could see that they were lying. On some occasions, friends took him to shrines to seek travel help, and several questions would be running through his head. *If he claims to be who he is, why haven't his conditions improved? Why is he still living in dilapidated houses and wearing rages, looking malnourished?*

It was all a waste of money and time, but he desired to see things personally and experience what others felt. He grew up in the church and never saw his parents go to fetish priests, but he was in another land filled with traditional beliefs. Ghana is home to rich culture and traditions. Seeking the face of another god who does not exist is such a waste of time and resources.

Programs were instituted by donor countries on humanitarian grounds allowing relatives and NGOs to assist residents of the United States and European countries to file applications for refugees' relatives to be repatriated to those countries on a resettlement program. The process was rigorous, which included a primary process to establish a family connection with anchor relatives filing such petitions and followed by interviews with foreign immigration officers to establish verification. It ended with a list of qualified candidates seeking admission who had successfully passed the immigration interview. Upon completing the process, you were required to go through medical testing conducted by a qualified health center chosen by those countries and that met international health standards. The program climaxed with weeks of orientation to avoid what was considered a cultural shock to refugees, informing them how the US society works and what to expect, including the importance of established local and federal laws, with benefits as well.

There were opportunities available for all, and friends did help a couple of others to get out and travel, for there were many without family abroad and depended on the generosity of others to survive. Men and women became beggars, and personalities were diminished because of the plight of being a refugee and having no means of generating income.

Clarence had tried many times to get a spot in the United States using different names and means but was not successful, no matter what he did. He lost hundreds of dollars for non-refundable charges paid to other family members and agents. The need to get out was important. Even with all the cash that he had; it was not his chosen time to get out.

When we become complacent in the sinful way of life, darkness is cast over the eyes of men, forbidding them to see the light. It is in such darkness that evil exists and causes one to become a slave to the devil. In such a period, he lost his sense of reasoning and became a leader of his own destiny. He made decisions out of ignorance because he was spiritually blind to the light of God while serving the devil and sharing a bed with the lust of this world. On one occasion, he even assisted a family of over twenty people, teaching them how the program works and writing their asylum story.

As time went by, he gave up on traveling abroad. Even when the right opportunity came, Clarence refused to travel under the disguise of another person's name. This time he told God, "If you need me to travel out of here, please let me use my biological name instead of anyone else's."

Thousands of refugees were qualified and left as if going to the land that was promised to the children of Israel. Folks were happy to leave the camp where safe drinking water was a serious problem. The camp had a halfway clinic with skeleton healthcare workers who were partly qualified to perform such duties. But they managed and settled in for what they had then; serious and other high health issues like diarrhea and waterborne were referred to larger hospitals thirty to fifty-five minutes away. Friends and families lost lives because of poor healthcare facilities, and residents of over fifteen thousand refugees had one ambulance that came on a certain day of the week.

Clarence became involved in lots of other income-generating initiatives and had to do everything necessary to stay on top of the game, as there were other competitors. The key here was to beat any price and secure the business with the client satisfied; it was a struggle to survive, and it became the survival of the fittest at times. He had the needed cash to decide and change the outcome of any game plan. They lived in a desperate time, and such times call for a desperate decision, but he was losing the game at the other end of life, familywise.

He had a grand-style wedding and married the love of his life in a rainbow ceremony.

After the wedding, things began to go downhill, and his wife got very ill and needed to see a physician. Then, he became so confused, and she had to be hospitalized for weeks under the observation of a doctor. Their daughter needed care and had to be with the mother while undergoing treatments. There was limited time to make ends meet. It was during those moments of desperation that he yielded to temptation by engaging in extramarital affairs. He had affairs with older and younger women who were all frustrated by the ongoing conflict taking place in their homeland. Some had escaped the brutalities of a civil conflict after witnessing some sort of violence and bloodshed. Others will tell stories of being tortured and raped by men of war. Parents would send their kids off to safety in neighboring countries just for survival.

It was all great at first with the absence of his wife as he wondered what was going wrong, and he needed his wife to return home and become the same person that she was. Later it was observed that his wife had been poisoned during the wedding by some unknown person. She had to be taken to another location for tribal healing, which lasted over a month. Through prayers and faith, she became healed and was transported home.

What do we do when faced with trials and tribulations? Who do we turn to in our times of need and uncertainties when all others have failed us? There will be days and nights of trials and sorry. At times, we might not be able to sleep and wonder what has taken place when our walls of Jericho would not fall. Do not give up but keep the faith and continue to trust in God.

*God is our refuge and strength, a
very present help in trouble.*
(Psalm 46:1)

Life continued afterward, and he sealed a friendship with the authorities and got the trust of a few friends who became local protectors. As time went by, the other side of business connections was failing, and he needed to supplement the income generation. He was introduced to another business through a friend who was an embalmer. His family had to be catered to, so Clarence became a handyman by learning a bit of every possible cash trade, which included carpentry, masonry, and embalming. The embalming issue was short but had fast cash by removing human remains and getting them to prepare for burial or transportation by air. The process was tedious and required lots of contacts to finally get custom papers of human remains exportation, among others. He had connections with the customs authorities and could navigate any hospital mortuary together with an embalmer who was under his contract. One thing they all had in common was the consumption of alcohol, which he knew very well and would not hesitate to purchase a few just to get the job going in the right direction. He was being paid and earned the middleman's share of the cash after such work was completed.

One thing that he learned from experience in dealing with humans is the fact that with all that we have here on the face of this earth, we shall one day return to our Creator naked as we came. It speaks volumes to know that man, with all the power and wealth, ends up being empty and lying cold in a freezer, naked. We need not be proud or selfish nor accumulate wealth on the face of this earth. We came empty and shall return as such. No matter how powerful we become on the face of the earth, the grave is a common place for the beggar, homeless, rich, and poor to rest without a class. This reminded him of what is written in the book of Psalm 90:12.

"So teach us to number our days,
that we may apply our hearts
unto wisdom."

As time went by, things began winding down, and Clarence decided to head back to his country of origin. The decision was not made lightly, but it was necessary for him to leave. As he slept that night, the thought of a new start began to flood his head. What could he do in a country that he had been absent for over ten years and where he barely had little or no contacts except his siblings?

Upon his return to his country of birth, he noticed that things had changed, and he could barely see his childhood friends. Some had been killed during the civil conflict, while others sought asylum in neighboring countries. Nevertheless, he was glad to be home, hoping to begin a new life and bury the flashbacks. The country of his birth made him confused as he wondered where to begin his new life. It was like placing a man in the midst of the jungle and instructing him to start a life without any equipment to begin. Clarence found his strength in playing the survival game, and he was good at networking with people. It took him weeks, and he began to make new friends and discovered the neighborhood's popular hangout places where folks met.

Chapter 7
YOU HAVE CANCER

*C*ancer has a name, but the name of Jesus is far greater than that name.

Regular walks on Saturday in the park were great for Clarence, as he would take that needed walk for one to three hours every weekend to keep healthy. There was no health concern at first that was bothering him except for common fatigue after regular walking or occasional soccer practice.

The usual weekend hanging with his crew of regular acquaintances who sat at a popular place of relaxation to discuss issues and petty gossip at times was important to him. The guys would play soccer and later sit under trees for hours having drinks. You could tell by the look on some faces that something was going on in their lives that needed to be addressed. But who was he to even tell them when faced with a dilemma of his own, trying to fight a devil within him? Indeed, a demon cannot drive out another demon, one would say; that is such a real saying. There was a light in him as had always been, but was he really using such light for its intended purpose, or was he trying to hide by avoiding what the higher calling was upon his life?

It was a nice Friday afternoon, and he stopped by his regular restaurant to get food from the Jamaican spot. He ordered oxtails and rice with peas. It was delicious. He ate and was filled and even added a ginger beer to cool it down. He sat for an hour or two after eating, conversing with a few others about the situation in their homeland. He bid them goodbye and left for home. He had been driving for twenty-five minutes and began feeling discomfort in his belly. What could he have eaten? He thought. It could not be the food because they cooked so well, and he had been eating there for years without a complaint. Besides, the restaurant score card was high, having passed the city inspection.

He got home, and the pain intensified within his belly, so much that standing was a problem, and it came with fever and chills too. He had to lie flat on the floor and cry for help, but he could not lie still for long as the pain was becoming unbearable. His health was taking a toll on him, and he began to grow tired throughout the evening. Prior to that, he had brought a plane ticket to visit his kids in Cherrytown and was wondering about missing the flight. "Should I call 911?" was the voice of his lovely wife asking, and he replied that she should not, that it would not take long.

There is this behavior when it comes to men seeing the doctor. They are constantly in a state of denial. Even when faced with medical concerns, they tend to put on the masculine suit of being in control and hiding pain. He had always looked forward to one thing at the end of the week, which was church service on Sunday, no matter what the situation might seem. Not satisfied with his current state of appearance, she took a cup of water that she had prayed over, mixed it with anointing oil, and gave him to drink, which he did. Later the pain subsided, and he was able to walk again gradually, but he was afraid and thought about what went wrong. He had learned to love Jesus early on and had begun to rely on Him for support through his chronic health issues. While he didn't have an official diagnosis, he did know that Jesus got him through some of the hardest situations of his life.

He knew he needed him more than ever. He had felt a new pain settling in his belly, and the fire had spread from his lungs to his skin. Every night, he was in agony, just trying to find rest. In a few days, he was up and ready to take his flight as planned, unaware of what was taking place within his body. This would have been a disaster for the kids and the other relatives, but the mercy of God kept him from falling. The visit to Cherrytown was a bitter-and-sweet moment; he felt something was wrong but could not comprehend what it was. He lost his sense of taste and felt nauseated at times but decided to take a shot of vodka as a remedy. The weekend was well spent, and he returned after having a heart-to-heart conversation with his older child, which was fruitful.

She drove him to the airport, and they said a prayer together, and she drove away with an agreement on what they had discussed in mind. Upon returning home, another friend had asked him to perform hand work and confirmed that it would be the next day because he had just returned from an outer state and needed to relax.

Early the next morning, he got up, took a shower, and headed out to perform the hand work. Heading out, the Holy Spirit directed him to the emergency section of the hospital for a check-up. The desk attendant asked him what his complaint was, and he initially lied by telling her about his heart just to be attended to early. While in the treatment room, he complained about his stomach. Blood samples were drawn out for further tests, and he was placed in a waiting room pending a doctor's availability.

After several hours, a female doctor finally entered the room and began to ask him a series of questions. She began by asking what brought him there and how the test showed no danger to his heart but that he needed emergency surgery. She asked if an ambulance drove him to the hospital, and he said no, his car was driven there. It seemed like his appendix had ruptured, but it could have been worse had the Holy Spirit never led him there. God had something planned that he was not aware of, and this is how he works behind the scenes, unknown to us.

After nearly six hours of being at the hospital, someone finally told me what was taking place behind the scenes during his long-awaited time. Later, an attendant brought in a wheelchair and took him to an assigned room upstairs, pending the surgical team's arrival. The surgeon finally arrived and requested that another CT scan be taken for clarity. Off he was taken by the transporter, as they were referred to at the facility.

Later in life, as we age and seem so energetic, there is always something in this world that is waiting there to remind us about how fragile we have become and that we are not immortal beings. Whether physical or spiritual, it is there to remind us of the one who is supreme and created us all. Everything seemed great though there were challenging times prior to the pandemic, but we managed to sail through the storms of life. Then came the pandemic when the world stood still and confused. News of death skyrocketed and shocked the entire broadcasting network, and one would get tired or even depressed about hearing and seeing pictures of corpses lying in the morgue while there were quite a few that must be put away on the burial grounds because there was no space. Human casualties were at an all-time high because of the outbreak of the corona virus, which would later be called COVID-19.

One would wonder if this was the end of the world, and for a moment or two, Clarence broke into tears, seeing people die and fight for life in the hospitals while health workers spent endless hours of work trying to control the situation. "Mankind has lost it all," he said. Despite the advancement of technology, we could not even control this pandemic. Where did we go wrong? Clarence sat and wondered what could be done to control the said situation. There were families weeping for their lost relatives. Grandparents and those with pre-existing conditions stood the greater risk of dying. "Is there a God up there?" people would say of the only man who held the answer to all our questions and the solution to the ongoing situation.

This was not his first surgery; if he could recall, this was the third one but the first on his belly. God had really been good to him, he wondered, despite those awful things that were done in the past year alone, cheating, lying, drinking, and the list was endless. Why would the Lord of hosts care for one sinner such as him and keep guarding his reckless life as he went on? There must be something that he saw in him, and because of His unfailing love for him, He does not want him to perish without fulfilling a mission.

Two weeks had gone by since the surgery, and it was time for a scheduled post-surgical visit with the surgeon. The clinic was narrow, and he had no insurance, but he knew that he would be seen since the surgery was performed without insurance. Upon arrival, he was escorted to a waiting room, and a nurse asked him to undress for the staples to be removed from his belly prior to the surgeon's appearance.

After all the staples were removed from his belly, the doctor appeared and began to ask about his feelings. He noted that all was well except for some minimum pain and sores from the stitches. "You will be all right," the doctor remarked, "but there is something that I must tell you, which is very crucial."

He took a seat and began to explain the result from the biopsy report, and at first, Clarence's mind was on the payment arrangement to cover the cost of the surgery. But what was coming would be a bombshell that he would forever remember. "You have cancer according to the report," stated the doctor, "and it is serious that I am recommending you see a specialist."

Clarence's world grew dark, and his legs gave up underneath him. "How bad is it?" he asked the doctor, "and how long do I have to live?" That he could not explain but instructed his aid to make a referral to a major hospital with a renowned specialist. Clouds of uncertainties began to flood his head, including fear. This was exactly what the devil wanted to use as his weapon against Clarence, "fear".

Whenever we are faced with situations that confuse us, we must realize that it is a spirit of deception. The enemies will manufacture lies and make us believe that there is no God and even try to put us in conditions where our faith in God is tested. Going through these trials will reaffirm our faith in God. James 1:2-4 tells us:

*"My brethren, count it all joy, when
you fall into diverse temptations;
know this, that the trying of your
faith worketh patience.
But let patience have her perfect
work, that you may be perfect
and entire, wanting nothing."*

"Every word spoken after that was meaningless to me," Clarence said as he began to reflect on his family. What would become of his children, as some were young and bonded to him? He couldn't work as many of his peers did because of his illness or perform community tasks. His health had taken a toll on him, and he had begun to grow tired throughout the day.

His love for Christ was never relinquished, and he trusted that God was going to show up for him in one way or another. So, he was not giving up, as this was just a test, no matter what the condition seemed like. While he didn't have an official diagnosis, he did know that Jesus got him through some of the hardest nights of his life. He knew he needed Him more than ever, as he felt new pain settling in his bones, and the fire had spread from his lower abdomen through his body. Every night, he was in agony, just trying to find rest.

He went outside and sat in the car, afraid to tell his wife because of fear that she might be worried, so he decided to call on a praying person, which was a mistake. He should have called on God first and then his servant, he later realized, but it was not too late. The servant of God remarked, "Let us give it to God," and told him to have faith. Thereafter, he told his wife, and she also said, "Clarence, cancer has a name, but the name of Jesus is above all names. It is in times like these when our faith and hope are tested that we call upon God for his grace."

The appointment was made, and he went to the hospital, unaware of what to expect from the specialist referral. Upon arrival at the facility, the specialist ordered that a CT scan be taken. He had developed tremors and blurred vision. He assumed it was hunger, but they suspected something more serious. He gave a kind-eyed nurse his history and explained that he didn't have insurance. She waved him away, seeming to understand his dire situation. He thanked God and sat, waiting for them to bring back a diagnosis.

Finally, the doctor came in. Her face was kind but profound, as if she had been doing this for far too long to have hope. "Clarence," she continued, "you have stomach cancer. That explains your symptoms, the fevers, and the bloody phlegm." He was floored. He looked at her stupidly, as if he was both deaf and dumb. "Cancer?" he asked.

During the consultation, she said to him, "You need surgery urgently."

"How bad is it," he asked her, "and can anything be done to reverse the situation?"

She explained in detail what the procedure would be like and advised that he should go ahead and do some reading on it prior to his next visit. She explained that the cancer had spread and was stage in four, but the surgery could reduce further spread. Option one of the procedure could last between six to ten hours, while option two would be eighteen hours, involving the removal of his intestine and the use of a bag outside his body.

He was speechless and wondered how this happened and what would become of him after such a procedure. She gave him a few days to think over what was discussed and call back to schedule the procedure. Then she asked, "Do you have an insurance?" He replied, "No." She requested the business office to put in an application for charity assistance, and the lady accepted it at once. God is great, as he later learned the hospital was going to be responsible for the entire procedure.

He began to discuss the procedure with family members and asked for privacy and faith in God, though the devil kept fear on his mind concerning the outcome of the surgery. During the week, he had a dream, and a lady appeared, telling him that the Lord said, "Trust him." Early the next morning, he woke up wondering what the dream meant. That was followed by a series of dreams about dead people. But there was a dream in which a dead woman of God anointed him, and the power of the Holy Spirit fell upon him.

He woke up early the next morning and said, "Lord, if there was ever a time that I doubted thee, please forgive and save me, for I trust in you alone." At night while praying, a family member fell under the anointing of the Holy Spirit and prophesied that God had spoken and said that whatever was about to be taken from his body was not coming back.

Clarence could barely sleep and kept thinking about the procedure and what life could be after. But God will never take us through any situation where he cannot save us. All we need to do is to put our trust in him and remind him of his words that say:

"Yea, though I walk through the valley
of the shadow of death,
I will fear no evil; for thou are with me;
thy rod and thy staff they comfort me."
(Psalm 23:4)

After this episode, he began to react differently by moving away from the social things of this life, becoming closer to the things of God, and even starting a media ministry where he administered the Word of God.

Finally, they arrived at 5:00 a.m. on the day of the surgery, and his wife bid him goodbye and left the facility as she was forbidden from entering because of COVID restrictions. This was a moment of uncertainty as no one knew what the next hour would hold, but his trust was in God as he headed into the operating room. If Clarence had forgotten everything said to him previously, one thing was certain on his mind, the voice from his dream: *Trust me,* which was said to him by the Lord of hosts. That was a sign that God was with him as promised because God never changes His words.

It wasn't that he couldn't bear the thought of dying; it was that he couldn't handle the thought of living onward, like not becoming who God wanted him to be. He didn't even know where he was headed anymore. He did the only thing he knew how to do once the pains had subsided, pray.

His heart was still somehow tender. He poured his heart out to God and begged Him for mercy. In his head, he had tumbled down the hill, tripping over a sharp rock. He did let his body roll and contort like a straw doll. He landed at the base of a clearing with beautiful savannah trees. He started crying all over again when he saw what was in front of him, realizing that it was all a dream.

Clarence entered the room, undressed as requested by the staff, and observed as they marked his personal belongings and put them away. Then the usual stuff followed: pre-op formalities by the nurses, and when the anesthesiologist came in and made an introduction after the surgeon had left, that was the last scene that he could remember. After ten hours, a nurse woke him up as he heard the voice saying, "Clarence, wake up the surgery was successful." He opened his eyes to behold tubes running all over his body while machines were connected, which made a slight sound. His belly was taped up, and his throat felt dried up. He requested a drink but was refused on the order of the surgeon. "I remained in such a position for two days," said Clarence, "being unable to move." On the third day, he was placed on a liquid diet, with nurses assigned to administer some medication every hour. Oh, how dreadful it was seeing nurses and doctors asking questions about how he felt. He only needed to rise and go down now. But with such a surgery, it was impossible. Days passed, and his diet restriction was downgraded to begin food intake but not solid food. "Only a watery diet for now," said the doctor to the nurses.

He inquired of the attendant when he would be permitted to leave the hospital, and she replied, "Once you can use the restroom frequently and walk without help." That did not seem like anytime soon, as the urge to use the restroom was far off. With tubes inserted in him and a portion of his intestine cut off, it was like starting life all over. But it was not over; as time went by, the urge to use the restroom began to increase, and his belly was also swelling. He remembered the surgeon coming in one morning and said, "Your stomach is twice what it should be like."

He was afraid and said, "Lord, I do not want another surgery. Please let this swelling go away." It is a painful situation when you have the urge to go but cannot, and your belly keeps hurting, thereby making you so uncomfortable. The pain was increasing, and the doctor prescribed medication to alleviate the situation, but it was to no avail. There is a saying that men do not cry, but that is just not true. Real men do cry out of shame or agony, but such is done in their quiet world.

He could remember crying to God that night, as he needed to ease the tension he faced. "Lord," he said, "I need you right now, please, because I just cannot take this any longer, and if this will lead you to take me, then, Lord, please take me home."

"I sought the LORD and he heard me
and delivered me from all of my fears."
(Palm 34:4)

Later that night, while lying on the bed, dosing off to sleep, he saw a nurse beside his bed, and she sat at the foot of his bed. She could feel his agony and said to him, "Clarence, try moving from left to right gradually." He replied that he could not move in the direction instructed. Afterward, something happened. She put her hands directly on his belly, and he began to move in the direction that the nurse had directed him. Within seconds, the urge to go was high. Afraid of messing up the room floor, he struggled to the bathroom, where, finally, he was able to release.

Upon return to the room, his assigned nurse came in and began to ask him if he was able to use the restroom. He replied in the affirmative, and the look on her face was that of surprise. "Were you in here a few minutes ago?" he asked, and she said no.

"What about the other nurses?"

She said, "I was sitting right outside the door and did not see anyone come through here." When she asked what had happened, he nodded and said, "Nothing, it's okay.

Clarence was pulled out of the valley to be used for God's glory. When in trials and situations where we cannot find hope and our faith seems to be shaken, there's a reminder that God is still on His throne. He will deliver us and set every believer free from the shackles of sin. Our God is the restorer of broken bridges, and He sets captives free. He answered prayer by fire. It is in this God that Clarence was taught to trust and fear and have faith in times of trouble. He had not changed. The God of grace had heard the prayer of a sinner and sent an angel to deliver him in his hour of desperation.

Clarence had just had an encounter with an angel who had touched him and healed his pain. The moment after the nurse left, a chill fell upon him, and he felt a strange presence in the room. At this moment, all he could do was accept the will of God, for at this point, it was either God's way or no way. He surrendered all and burst into tears, crying like a child who had lost his mother. He opened to the will of God and said, "I am yours, Lord; use me for your glory because I have seen it all and want nothing less than to love you even more." This is what an encounter with God can do to people. It places you at a point to surrender, especially if you have been running away from the calling to serve Christ. God will meet you at a point where you will have no option but to surrender to his will.

"Take my yoke upon you and learn of
me; for I am meek and lowly in heart:
and ye shall find rest unto your souls"
(Mathew 11:29)

There are times when God will put us in certain conditions just to claim our attention because we are too busy to acknowledge Him. It is not the will of the Father to allow evil and tribulation to fall upon us, but He uses these situations to test our faith in Him and see how much trust we can place in Him. Going through pain and uncertainties while under the knives, Clarence was sure of one that God was faithful to His words of delivering him for His glory.

After two weeks in the hospital, he was discharged and left for home, but he could barely walk by himself and needed help moving around the house. A cane was brought to assist him in moving around the house when the folks had gone to work. Loneliness is a terrible thing to experience, while living among family is the greatest gift of life amongst all. Take some time to cherish your loved ones and family members while you have the time, for such time is promised to no man. Always try to appreciate the laughter and care while you can, for when the waves of life and storms of life try to fall in, you will have such an anchor to lean on as they roll in. Learn to hold hands and pray together as one, for prayer changes everything to those who believe in whom they pray. Accept each other for your individual faults while trying to forgive and seek means that will hold such a union together and not destroy it. "I have seen families have a reunion at the graveyard sites," Clarence said, "because of hatred, pride, and selfishness. If we just forgive and let bygones be bygones, limit or desist from the little lies and gossip that tear families and communities apart, it will be a great world."

During his recovery, Clarence experienced more post-surgical pain. While trying to heal, he noticed that he could barely walk and had no strength in his legs to even hold him up. But he kept the faith, unable to speak or have free bowel movements because of the extreme pain that accompanied the surgery. Gradually, he tried to recover but was afraid to eat because of the nature of the pain he experienced. It was during such time that his faith grew even stronger, having survived such an ordeal and knowing that there was a cause for going through it.

God was just starting with him, but to realize his fulfillment, he had to go through the moment to gain his redemption. Salvation is a gift given to every one of us, but it is also not cheap, lest anyone take it for granted. God is willing to forgive and give a second, even third chances if time permits, but we must also be willing to make a commitment and be sincere in our requests.

Within two months after the surgery, he had another appointment to visit for chemotherapy treatment. The surgeon had recommended three rounds, but after consultation, the specialist in charge recommended five treatments for six months.

Cancer is the name of a beast that robs our homes, takes away families and loved ones, and leaves us devastated with many unanswered questions. But we heard about another name, and this time around, the name of Jesus Christ was a higher tower that the righteous ran to and be rescued.

During the first visit, he was a bit frightened. There are times when we become afraid and neglected. At that moment, you are about to experience a feeling that no one will ever understand but you and your God. What the body was about to go through will forever be remembered for as long as he lives. At the treatment center, you could see the faces of patients who had been diagnosed with cancer and wondered how they felt. Whatever those feelings were, it was not happy one at all, and one need not ask why, as the expression on those faces was a complete narrative of what they felt.

110

Only those who undergo chemotherapy can explain the feeling of such, and the reaction from every individual is different. How can you tackle such a topic as cancer when you have never traveled the path as a cancer patient? There were days and nights when he could barely sleep, with chemicals running for an additional seventy-two hours from a pump after every three-hour treatment for six months. He had lost every feeling of being an active person, including the loss of appetite because of a sore mouth from the chemo and weakness. Clarence narrated how he could recall the awful sound of the chemo pump at night, and the task of carrying it, strapped to his body. Of course, he did not forget the night sweats too, and the feeling that his body was overheating at times. He wondered how this was all going to play out.

According to the doctor, the treatment was to prevent the reoccurrence of cancer. But the faith that Clarence relied on was the voice of God saying that it is not coming back! *There are times in our lives when we put our trust in a place where faith cannot find itself; then, we must lean and depend on a higher power to lead us through.* At this point, he depended only on the promises of the higher God to lead him through to the end of the chemo session. There were stories told of folks who did not make it through to the end of chemo sessions. Some died early while undergoing chemo due to complications or preexisting conditions. Others would suffer liver damage, among other underlying reactions, for life because of the toxic nature of the chemical agents which were deposited into the person's body.

Several months after the chemo treatment, he was sent for a routine CT scan by the surgeon, and when the scan results were in, the doctor stated that there was no need for concern. *What did she mean?* Clarence thought as he reflected on the pre-diagnosis given earlier by the doctor. *Was it that the disease had been treated to a minimum or controllable level, raising no need for concern, or that it was eliminated by God as promised?*

Not satisfied with the physician's assistant explanation, Clarence decided to speak directly with the surgeon by sending her an email. Later, she called back and apologized, giving a reason why she could not be present at his prior appointment but that the CT scan showed no evidence of cancer at all.

It is a miracle that stage four cancer had been healed and is not coming back as God has said. Our faith in God is constantly tested by works, which include surviving to the end of every situation that appears to hold us down. Disappointments and diseases, among other things, were not made as a life sentence for us but, at times stepping stones to climb higher and reach our potential in life.

There are some who may sit and try to judge God when faced with situations because of their limited minds, but the power of God exceeds our expectations. He is our Creator and does not need permission to act slowly or quickly, but He will do whatever has been promised in our lives at His appointed time. Through Clarence's pain and frustration, his love and trust for God grew even more to the point that he gave up and surrendered in total submission to the will of God. Clarence remembers saying, "Here I am, Lord. Use me only for your glory; even send me wherever you need me." When we pray and do not get an instant reply from God, there are reasons for His delay. It should not be taken as a sign of denial but as a period of waiting until you receive the expected call, which might not be an easy thing to do. God will always keep His words and promises given to us. Despite our disobedience, He still loves us.

At the end of the chemotherapy session, Clarence needed to recover what was taken away by the treatment. Vitamins, energy, and temporary memory loss were all the feelings he experienced. Here is a good piece of advice for those who have gone through some sort of chemotherapy treatment. Modern medications are changing because of ongoing cancer research treatment. Thinking creatively will also help one to recover quickly just by carefully selecting your diet and consuming natural nutrition. Gaining the needed strength, appetite, and weight will be a gradual process, but you will need to keep focus. Exercise regularly and stay committed to both your medical team and nutritionist. Pray constantly while keeping your faith in God, for He is a deliverer in times of trouble. Find a support group of people who share your feelings, have similar experiences, and will pray alone with you. Avoid being alone because cancer is a killer, and you do not want to sink further. Healing is available. Trust God; He will never fail you, and in the end, your healing will become such a testimony that prayer and faith go together.

A house on a beautiful rock, flat, completely empty, with a side garden, fresh fruits, fresh veggies, and a small well was his house on the rock. Thank you, God. Somehow, by faith alone, he had escaped death. He cried with relief. His tears flowed down his face like waterfalls of sadness and joy as he remembered the beautiful look of the girl who got shot on his back porch. He whispered a quiet prayer for her soul and those kids who had earlier passed unto eternity for keeping them under his wings, safe from angry men of war.

Clarence

"Everyone then who hears these words of mine
and does them will be
like a wise man who built his house on the rock.
And the rain fell, and
the floods came, and the winds blew and beat on
that house, but it did
not fall, because it had been founded on the rock."
(Matthew 7:24-25)

Made in the USA
Columbia, SC
25 May 2023

16920060R00074